2009 Poetry Competi[…]

I have a dream 2009

Words to change the world

Martin Luther King

John Lennon

South & South West England

Edited by Vivien Linton

First published in Great Britain in 2009 by:

Young Writers
Remus House
Coltsfoot Drive
Peterborough
PE2 9JX
Telephone: 01733 890066
Website: www.youngwriters.co.uk

Book Design by Spencer Hart & Tim Christian

SB ISBN 978-1-84924 380 3

Foreword

'I Have a Dream 2009' is a series of poetry collections written by 11 to 18-year-olds from schools and colleges across the UK and overseas. Pupils were invited to send us their poems using the theme 'I Have a Dream'. Selected entries range from dreams they've experienced to childhood fantasies of stardom and wealth, through inspirational poems of their dreams for a better future and of people who have influenced and inspired their lives.

The series is a snapshot of who and what inspires, influences and enthuses young adults of today. It shows an insight into their hopes, dreams and aspirations of the future and displays how their dreams are an escape from the pressures of today's modern life. Young Writers are proud to present this anthology, which is truly inspired and sure to be an inspiration to all who read it.

Contents

The Ridgeway School, Wroughton

Treviglas Community College, Newquay

Wareham Middle School, Wareham

Wiltshire College, Salisbury

The Poems

Future

The future will have children smarter
Who like to play and like to have fun
Fossil fuel hunting stops and solar power comes in
Cars will be flying, buildings will be higher.

Teenagers will graduate, opening them to the big wide world
Some cars will still have wheels, but will have
solar or wind power propellers with wings
Trains having double speed and stronger brakes
Public pathways will be extra parking for flying cars
The public will have jet packs over their heads
That have Sat Nav built in and jet rockets blasting.

More grass will grow as houses are hovering above the ground
Robots will form and serve the humans
Starships will cruise in space for holidays beyond imagination
Passenger planes with seven star ratings
Military weapons with 100% accuracy
The Royal Air Force fighter jets advanced
Cruise ships will sail underwater
Battleships will be stealth ships.

Babies will grow to children, teenagers
Adults and elderly
Who have experienced the world.

The future is now
And it's up to you.

James Fowler (13)
Bovington Middle School, Wareham

Some Day

In the future
Close your eyes and imagine

Some day you'll wake up
The sun will shine brightly
This is the future

Some day they'll give up
War as we know it will end
This is the future

Some day they'll stop waste
Then global warming will end
This is the future

Some day you'll learn
And discover new things
This is the future

Some day we'll find cures
No one will get sick again
This is the future

Today is yesterday's future
And tomorrow is yours
Go ahead and make a difference.

Kaitlin McNeil (12)
Bovington Middle School, Wareham

I See A Day

I see a day
Not long into the future
Where the grass is greener
And the sea is bluer

I see a day
Not long into the future
Where war is stopped
And gang fights are gone

I see a day
Not long into the future
Where poverty has left
And disease does not spread

I see a day
Not long into the future
Where everyone is smiling
And nobody is unhappy

I see a day . . .
        I see a day . . .
                I see a day.

Nicky Hocking (13)
Bovington Middle School, Wareham

Better Place

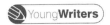

These salty, salty tears,
Running from my eyes,
Running down my neck,
Right down to my thighs,
Life's not worth this pain,
Life's not worth these cries,
The world has gone evil,
An hour a hundred dies,
The world is full of blasphemy,
The world is full of lies,
All that people do,
Is try to criticise,
Won't you take one second?
To try to visualise,
A world full of love and peace,
Just try to emphasise,
The good things in life,
Maybe we could compromise,
With all of the bad,
Maybe we could minimize,
All of the terrible crime,
Maybe we could reduce all of the demise,
Then the world would be a better place.

Chalaina Brewer (13)
Clarendon College, Trowbridge

I Have A Dream

I have a dream to be in a team
I have a dream that I can build big things
I have a dream to be a millionaire
I have a dream to be an astronaut
I have a dream that my family will live forever
I have a dream about all these things and more.

Rhys Collier (13)
Devizes School, Devizes

I Have A Dream!

I have a dream!
The world will get smarter
Civilisation will improve
There will be new words in the dictionary
Money will reach the trillions
And blacks will be welcome wherever they are in the world.

I have a dream!
That children won't be abused by their parents
And cancer will be cured
There will be no racism
This is my dream and I'm sticking by it.

I have a dream!
Children will be born with no problems
They will be looked after
They won't be abused
They'll turn out great, powerful
And in control of their actions
And parents will think twice before hurting a child.

I have a dream!
Global disasters will be fixed by new order
Science will fix the diseases in the air
People will open their minds more
Before resorting to violence or murder.

I have a dream!
Terrorism has got to stop
We must act against terrorism and violence
And violence in the world
But with men in the world, there will be war
If we don't act now
We will start World War III
And start at the beginning with sticks and stones
My dream is that it must stop now.

Hugh Goodier (14)
Devizes School, Devizes

I Hope You Could Be Here Today

He died when I needed him the most,
It's like a damaged duck stranded on a coast.
He was like family and a friend,
What I thought was until the end.
When I was little, I thought it would last forever,
What me and him shared together.
But then when I saw Mum crying,
He wasn't there, because he was dying.
I felt upset and sick inside,
No one was there to help me decide.
I came home to find the house phone ringing
And when it did, my heart was singing.
But then it was him saying his goodbyes
And that's when I assumed it was all lies.
I hung up and sat down, crying,
Then realised he wasn't lying.

A few days later, people dressed in black,
Crowded in the cemetery, crying on each other's back.
All I wanted was to get them to tell
And as they did, their eyes started to swell.

The days since then have been hard
And every birthday I write him a card.
Not that he gets it, not that he'll see,
What I want to grow up and be.
Sometimes I remember in my mind,
What he was like, nice and kind.
I remember when things were good, not bad,
But now everyone is depressed and sad.

Since you've been gone, things have changed,
Dad's disappeared and Mum's gone strange.
Dad divorced and moved away
And I hope I'll see him again or today.
Mum has moved on, there are no more fights
And now we can go see lots of sights.
Even though I wish you were there,
I know you're still watching, I hope you still care.

Life is different now that you're gone,
But time will heal, as life moves on
And now that I've finished, all there is left to say,
Is I hope you could be here today.

Mollie O'Sullivan (13)
Devizes School, Devizes

Imagine

Imagine there are no people
Imagine they are all dead
Imagine there's no blue sky
Imagine it's fiery red

I have a dream to do everything
I have a dream to be everything
I have a dream to see everything
I have a dream to win everything

Imagine there's no wildlife
Imagine they are all dead
Imagine there's no Earth
Imagine it's like crumbled bread

What if all these things happened?
Would everything be dead?
Would the sky turn fiery red?
What if there was no Earth?
It's crumbled like bread

All these things could happen
It could happen to us
When we're not expecting it
It could be in a blush

All these good things that we have done
Careless polluters could kill us all
They are all reckless idiots
Who don't make a fuss
Who couldn't give one tick about us.

Bryn Drewett (12)
Devizes School, Devizes

Mum

My mum, my mum
I love her to bits
My mum, my mum
We really do fit
My mum, my mum
I always wear her gloves
My mum, my mum
We're like two doves.

My mum, my mum
She buys me loads of clothes
My mum, my mum
She's got a weird nose
My mum, my mum
She makes me laugh
My mum, my mum
She keeps slipping down the path
And oh my, she makes me laugh!

My mum, my mum
No matter what you do
I'll always be there for you
My mum, my mum
You're the best thing that's ever happened to me
My mum, my mum
You know where I am if you need me
My mum and me, we're like two doves
And we will always be in love.

My mum, my mum
I love you to bits
My mum, my mum
She's a bit of a wimp
My mum and me we're like two pimps.

My mum, my mum
She's scared of spiders
But so am I!
My mum, you'll always be in my heart
And I will love you forever and ever

And nothing, absolutely nothing
Can break that.

Amy Glover (13)
Devizes School, Devizes

How To Inspire

If you're old, short or clever
And don't give up, no matter the weather,
Believe in your dreams,
Even if they rip at the seams,
Your name will be remembered forever.

Becky Hanney (14)
Devizes School, Devizes

Look Outside

Look outside, what do you see?
Children being abused by their families,
Stood outside in the dark, cold streets,
Wondering how they're going to survive.

Look outside, what do you smell?
Children smoking, adults too
Doing damage to themselves
And to others too.

Look outside, what do you hear?
Drunken people being stupid
Like shouting and swearing
Then an ambulance comes along
They get yet another casualty in A and E
Even if it is full up.

Look outside, what do you taste?
People being bullied, teased and hurt
Just because they're who they are.

Look outside, what do you feel?
Gangs going around vandalising your facilities
Without a care in the world.

Look outside, what do you see, hear, taste, smell, feel?
This is our world tumbling down
Why and how on earth did we let the world get like this?
I don't know about you
But I don't want to live in a world like this
So let's help make our world a better place
Seriously, it's worth it.

Molly Dilling (12)
Devizes School, Devizes

We Are All Different - No One Is The Same!

You and me are completely different,
Different minds, different personalities, different souls,
You and me are completely different,
Different achievements, different dreams, different goals.

As we stand, hand in hand,
We realise we are all equal,
As we stand, hand in hand,
We will help each other, even when we fall.

You and me are completely different,
Different minds, different personalities, different souls,
You and me are completely different,
Different achievements, different dreams, different goals.

We will come together as one,
Under the same sun, walking on the same land,
We will come together as one,
Through the sea and on the sand.

You and me are completely different,
Different minds, different personalities, different souls,
You and me are completely different,
Difference achievements, different dreams, different goals.

It doesn't matter what we look like,
We are always going to be friends,
It doesn't matter what we look like,
Together forever 'til the very end.

You and me are completely different,
Different minds, different personalities, different souls,
You and me are completely different,
Different achievements, different dreams, different goals.

Lily Shergold (12)
Devizes School, Devizes

My Pet Poem

My lovely lady Lily cat
Is as sweet as a lily pad
But she can be as scary as a tiger
She loves to play all day
And enjoys a home to stay
She may have been taken from her family
But she loves us all and we love her.

My beautiful Blue boy is very sweet
He loves to lay in the sun and eat all day
He loves to hunt for mice
But he really is a great big softie inside
I love the way his whiskers are
And I love it when he snuggles up beside me in the night.

My brilliant Bunny boy is so grumpy in the mornings
But is always happy during the day
I love the way they call him a lion head
Because he has a great big fluffy mane
When he is in the garden, he loves to play with his footballs
When it is very hot, he sits inside his tunnels.

My pretty Pippy boy is very skitty
But he loves us all
And in the day he loves to eat the juicy carrots that I give him
When he is with Bunny, he loves to play football with him
He may be small, but he has a big heart inside of him
And that is why we love him.

I hope you liked reading all about my pets
But I can't judge who is the best
Because they are all going to stay with me, in my heart, together
They will always look over me
Because they love me from the bottom of their little hearts.

Alexandra Searle (12)
Devizes School, Devizes

A Fab Poem

Cesc Fabregas,
Plays for Arsenal,
Attacking midfielder,
Goal sealer,
So say great,
Doesn't wear number eight.

Cesc Fabregas,
Plays under Wenger,
Who sometimes is a little winger,
Cesc's teammates,
Don't get good rates,
With rubbish like Eboue and Gallas,
But greats like Arshavin and Cesc Fabregas.

Cesc Fabregas,
Came from Spain,
Where he played for Barca,
A long time ago,
He played with the likes of Ronaldinho.

Cesc Fabregas,
Is world class,
Better than Gerrard or Ronaldo,
Don't know about Zinadine Zidane though.

Cesc Fabregas,
Is the one,
Who will get Arsenal winning games that come,
Winning Champion's Leagues
And the Premier League,
So Man Utd watch out,
Because Cesc Fabregas is about to be let out.

Harry Lewis (11)
Devizes School, Devizes

Keep On Looking . . .

Love will come,
Love will go,
But a broken heart,
Cannot be sewn,
So try to find the one,
Who will help you heal,
Who will stay true,
Who is completely real,
They will help you see,
The world through new eyes,
Your only soulmate,
They shall never tell lies,
They will keep their promises,
Through thick and thin,
Whatever the weather,
Through rain and wind,
There is only one,
Who can save your heart,
There is only one,
From whom you will never part,
They are out there,
You'll find them one day,
The perfect person who,
Will take your breath away.

So keep on looking
And you will find,
Who you've been waiting for,
All your life.

Maddie Pearce (12)
Devizes School, Devizes

Imagine

Imagine all the people
Imagine what they do
Imagine how they do it
Imagine you could do something too

Imagine who you could help
Imagine what you could do
Imagine burning flames in your eyes
Imagine what they would do though

Imagine all their injuries
Imagine how they feel
Imagine all the pain they suffer
Imagine if that was you

Imagine who they meet
Imagine who they know
Imagine how they do it
Imagine why they do it though

Imagine all the violence
Imagine all the blood
Imagine all the pain they feel
Imagine if they were too late

Now this is my dream
To help these people
Before it's too late
Imagine what you could do.

Dan White (13)
Devizes School, Devizes

The World Comes Alive

The world comes alive

Everywhere I look, I see,
The daffodils growing as spring approaches,
The soft, white clouds drifting slowly apart,

The world comes alive

Everywhere I turn, I hear,
The waves crash against the rough rocks,
Children laughing in the background,

The world comes alive,

Everywhere I walk, I feel,
The cool breeze brush past my face,
The warm sun beaming upon myself,

The world comes alive

Everywhere I go, I smell,
The salty air filling my nostrils,
The freshly cut grass,

The world comes alive

Everywhere I step, I taste,
The long awaited ice cream,
The sweet taste of doughnuts tickling my tastebuds,

The world comes alive.

Georgina Drewitt (13)
Devizes School, Devizes

Tick-Tock

I didn't ask to be swept along with the tide,
It's so strong and in this ocean there's nowhere to hide.

Life is moving, hurtling, spiralling
And we're supposed to be sat ready for this ride,
Like a great white startling its prey, no warning,
Everyone's watching,
Everyone's holding their breath.

No one really knows,
How this life is supposed to go.
Do we follow the days on the calendar?
Do we follow the numbers of the clock?
What if one day, everything just stopped?

We'll look at the sky to tell us the time,
We'll look at the trees to tell us the season,
Then we'll look and see the reason
How our lives can have more freedom.
Is it worth living inside this clock, deemed to run out of time?

To escape to the Kalahari,
Where nothing is of value,
Except for life, water and family.
This is my dream,
That the world will come out to play,
To stop reality, just for a day.

Clare Balmer (18)
Devizes School, Devizes

A Wonderful World!

I have a dream that one day everybody
Will be civil to each other in every way.
I have a dream that every child will not be beaten
And will live in every way that they should be treated.
I have a dream that people will not kill one another
And will be blood brothers until they die.

I have a dream that children shall live
And will blow out their first birthday candle.
I have a dream that everyone will not be racist
On both black and white people and cause lots of terrorism.

I have a dream that there is no violence
With guns and knife crimes on the streets we live in.
I have a dream there is no suffering or children in poverty
I have a dream that people should live in a place
They deserve to live in.

I have a dream that the world will be at peace
And will not be destroyed into little pieces.
I have a dream that men shouldn't beat
Women and children black and blue.

I have a dream that the world would live in harmony
And will not be controlled by selfish people
That they don't deserve to have.

Corianne Barratt (13)
Devizes School, Devizes

I Have A Dream

I have a dream
That the world would be complete with harmony,
Where blokes don't beat women black and blue,
Just think, it could be you,
What do you want to do?
Blokes have more power than you.

David Hockney (14)
Devizes School, Devizes

To The People

People weep when they lose
People weep about their loss
Why should we play if the stakes are high?
War is the game and we will die
The Earth is falling over itself
All we do is make more guns to kill
To fight the innocent ones
We need to stop, to help ourselves
Or say goodbye and hello to Hell
Our people fall, our people die
Those people are real heroes
To give their life for our country
But why should we fight and struggle?
If our ancestors saw us now
Then they would sure slap us from Heaven to Hell
The ten pound note, it isn't really money
The ten stands for the men's lives
That have died for that evil piece of paper
We should remember those men that have fallen
And stop those who are
Our people are at risk
But remember still who you are
You belong to your country.

Chris Connor (13)
Devizes School, Devizes

Mother Teresa

T he mother of all children
E ndless love to all
R emembering the good times
E verlasting friendships
S urviving the bad times
A gainst all the odds.

Adam Walters (13)
Devizes School, Devizes

I Have A Dream

I have a dream
That one day people will talk to each other
And walk together like brothers
With no fighting or war just because of their religion
Or for who they are.
I have a dream
That one day people are equal in every way
And they share all the land and treat each other
Like they are from the same brotherhood.
I have a dream
That one day all man-made weapons will be destroyed
And instead, there will be a weapon of peace
Because violence is not the answer to war
Peace is the new word.
I have a dream
That one day the world will be populated
By all the men and women from forces
Who would not have to fight and would live
And they would live a happy life with their families
Or do things that they would never have been able to do
One person dying of old age
Would be the same as 100 people dying in war.

Harry Wells (14) & Josh Wakefield
Devizes School, Devizes

Lewis Hamilton

Lewis Hamilton, Lewis Hamilton
Races around
Silverstone racing track

Silverstone, Silverstone
Is covered in rain, covered in rain
Now his car is in parts
He can have a jam tart.

Ryan Locke (12)
Devizes School, Devizes

RIP Paul

Why did it start?
Why did it happen?
Why to him?
No one forgiven!

He followed his dreams,
Heart and soul
And died in the war,
Vulnerable and outdoors.

His brother, Leon,
Saw through the war,
On compassionate leave,
To be there for him.

Friends and family,
Dearly missed by many,
Inspiring people
To follow their dreams,
Don't be *afraid!*
The light at the end,
Will put you through.

Love you, Paul.

Emily Young (14)
Devizes School, Devizes

Time

Live every day like it's your last,
Everything else is in the past,
Make friends in the present,
Before the moon is in its crescent,
In the future the world will change,
You and me would find it strange,
So live every day like it's your last,
Soon it'll all be in the past.

Chloe Scott (14)
Devizes School, Devizes

Myself . . .

They want me to be a chav,
They want me to be a Goth,
But
I want to be me!

They want me to be posh,
They want me to be glamorous,
But
I want to be me!

They want me to be trendy,
They want me to be smart,
But
I want to be me!

They want me to be quiet,
They want me to be loud,
But
I want to be me!

I wish to be free
I want to be me
But they won't let me be
I want to be myself!

Imogen Spurrell (12)
Devizes School, Devizes

I Believe

I believe that every child deserves a home
And deserves food and water.
I believe that every animal has a right to have a home
And is not to die by people cutting down their habitats.
I believe that every child should have a proper education
And know how to read and write
And I believe that Gandhi's words were right
'That an eye for an eye, makes the whole world go blind'.

Sarah King (12)
Devizes School, Devizes

Stop Bullies

Bullies
The ones that wait
In the playground
For you

Bullies
The ones that make
Your stomach turn
Before school

Bullies
The ones that give you bruises
On your arms and legs
Or even inside

Bullies
The ones that make you
Pretend
That everything's fine

Bullies
The ones we could be
If you told
Stand up for yourself!

Rachel Poole (12)
Devizes School, Devizes

9/11

So many lives lost
So many people died
People fought for other people
But they all tried their best to get through it
The plane and the people tried their best
They all went to Heaven for their rights
And let's keep it that way for helping.

Elliot Haywood (11)
Devizes School, Devizes

Kate And Me

Kate and me
Best mates we'll be
We'll cherish the moments
For always, you and me

We'll be together
And no matter what, we'll always have each other
Our friendship will be deeper than the sea
For always, you and me

We've had our ups and downs
But we got up every time we hit the ground
Not giving a what or who about what happened
For always, you and me

Kate and me are such good mates
Sometimes we hate each other
But most of the time, we love each other
For always, you and me

Kate and me
Best mates we'll always be
We'll never forget the cherished moments
For always, you and me.

Pritika Patel (14)
Devizes School, Devizes

My Mummy

My mummy is the bestest,
Because she is my mum
And I'll tell you one thing,
She's a great big ball of fun!

I could not imagine,
Being mummy-less,
It makes me kinda upset
But I know that she's the best.

She feeds me in the morning,
She feeds me in the night,
We hardly every disagree
And we never, ever fight.

She overlooks my bad mistakes,
She rights me when I'm wrong,
She never needs to tell me off,
She used to sing me songs.

That's why my mummy is the best
But if you've got a question
I'm sure we'd be able to work it out
But in Miss Saunders' detention!

Hannah Stradling (12)
Devizes School, Devizes

Follow Your Dreams!

President Obama
Inspired me because
A black president
There never ever was

Just look at his good ideas
And they are actually true
He says what he means
What he is willing to do

So now maybe this poem
Has turned your life around
It has brought it up from a nosedive
And saved it from hitting the ground

It has told you
You can do anything
If you put your mind to the test
You can dance, you can act, if you really want to, sing

Do not let any superior
Tell you what you can't do
Get up there and show them
And show the whole world too.

George Kelly (12)
Devizes School, Devizes

A Dream

A world where there is peace, not hatred,
Where every child can live without fear
And can play untroubled and protected,
To never shed a tear.

A world where black and white are equal,
Where we are all brothers under the skin,
Religion doesn't divide us,
But truth will always win.

A world where polar bears can wander,
Without fear of melting ice,
Where the rainforest is protected,
Now wouldn't *that* be nice!

A world where fighting is a myth,
No need for guns or knives,
Where we walk, arm in arm,
Without fear for our lives.

A world where beauty is all around us,
No ugliness or woe,
Yes, it could be Heaven,
But a world we will never know.

William Musgrove (13)
Devizes School, Devizes

Rivers, Oceans, Mountains And Fields

Rivers and stream run through the land belonging to the Earth,
The water as clear and clean as the blue sky
On a hot summer's day,
As chilled as a fridge to cool you down,
As quiet as a mouse in its deep sleep.

Oceans and seas fill the Earth with blue,
Waves crashing against the spiked rocks on the coast,
Roaring as loud as a lion battling the fast striking lightning
On a stormy day,
Then suddenly, it all falls dead and silent.

Mountains and hills rest high in the sky,
Relaxed, lonely and so very still,
Seeing the world at a point that no man can reach,
Warm, windy and very welcoming,
They have the beauty of the rose, as if it were carved by angels.

Fields and farms where hard men work,
The sun shining to help things grow,
Children running as fast as rain falls from the heavens,
Flying kites in the cold breezy wind,
Families having picnics on a hot sunny day.

Fay Benfield (14)
Devizes School, Devizes

Our World

Think of rain as drops of joy
Giving life to plants
And wind as the breath of angels
Blowing worries away

Spread peace and happiness
Over the world like butter over toast
Let the sun shine respect over the world
Love our world!

Harriet Allen (12)
Devizes School, Devizes

C'mon You Reds!

I love to play football,
I also love to watch,
The team I support is Man United,
They play at Old Trafford,
In a strip of bright red.

They really are the best,
As a team, they're ahead of the rest.

There's Rooney, who is ace,
At striking and hitting the net
And Ronaldo who is quick with his feet
And likes to head in the goals,
Then Ferdinand and Vidic,
Are rocks in defence.

The manager is great,
Alex Ferguson is his name,
He's led the team to Wembley,
Time and time again,
We've won many cups
And if we ever went down,
I'm sure we'd come right back up.

Jordan Allen (12)
Devizes School, Devizes

I Have A Dream . . .

I have a dream, that on a bright summer's day,
All colours will sit in the sun.
On the 11th of May,
Rights and opinions for everyone.

This world should be a free, loving place,
Where faiths and religions shake hands,
Smiles and laughter on every face,
The rich and poor share land.

Tessa-Louise Haines (12)
Devizes School, Devizes

Untitled

The red leather sphere
Skims off the edge
Of the slim, wooden bat
It soars through the air
Like a fish racing upstream
As it descends the player leaps
Desperately
Trying to read the ball
The crowd roars
As it sinks
Slow motion like
Into his nervous hands
He catches it
The match closes
And slowly beats
To a stop
The players walk off
They know
That unlike the cricket ball
There are some things in life
You cannot hold onto forever.

Oliver Savill (12)
Devizes School, Devizes

Poem

A world with no hunger
Would be good
Plenty of water
Plenty of food

Sweets would be pointless
Chocolate too
Beef, potatoes, rice
And vegetables would do.

Robin Gardiner (13)
Devizes School, Devizes

Eternity

Our world is our home and our battlefield
We fight, we play and we love
Our world is soon going to crumble down
We will die and we will drown
It's our turn to turn it around
Climate change is more than a myth
It is real and is killing our world
It is caused by us and us alone
I do not want to take care of it on my own
Get out there and save our planet
My role model is Al Gore
He believes that we should be grateful
For the things we have right in front of us
He gets a message across to the people of this world
I just hope you find that message in my writing
Find your heart, find your soul
You should now know giving up on the human race is not an option
Think of others before yourself
And thrive to succeed in the mission
To make sure life here is safe, good and most of all
For eternity.

Emily Hutchinson (12)
Devizes School, Devizes

Role Models!

Role models have to be strong,
Very powerful and brave too,
But sometimes they are wrong,
Just like me and you!

People look up to others,
Sometimes it's your mother,
I look up to my mum,
Because she's number one!

Laura Godwin (12)
Devizes School, Devizes

Does Tomorrow Ever Come?

To change the world around us, give it what you have
And serve it with what you may be.
When you walked into my life,
You brightened the stars,
It's like the knife has been lifted out of my heart.
Love of my life, my soulmate,
You're my best friend.
Why have I only just found you?
So many times have passed
And still our love will last.
We're together through the good times and the bad,
My heart's pumping like it's mad.
As if it were an uncontrollable feeling that wouldn't ever end,
That's the way you make me feel.
My life now is so real,
The fire that burned was once in my heart alive
And now finally, it has died.
Let our souls join as one,
As our new life has begun . . .
Together, forever and always,
Tomorrow has finally come!

Tayler Hayden (13)
Devizes School, Devizes

I Have A Dream

I have a dream,
To be seen,
When I'm older,
I'm going to be an actress.

Imagine that lovely mansion,
Imagine meeting a celeb,
Imagine that hot tub,
Imagine everyone wanting your autograph.

Bethany Powell (12)
Devizes School, Devizes

Formula 1

Formula 1 is great
Formula 1 is fun
I like to watch it with my mum.

Formula 1 is exciting
Formula 1 is fast
Formula 1 is brilliant
When the cars go zooming past.

The crowd are crazy
The roaring engines loud
When I see my team win
It makes me very proud.

The track is really buzzing
The cars go round real fast
Everybody's happy
Except the guy who's last.

The race is now over
The champagne cork has been popped
Hamilton wins the race
And now he is the top!

Jack Wright (14)
Devizes School, Devizes

Racism

No matter what skin or religion,
Everyone's the same,
So no matter what person,
Even though they look and sound different,
They should be treated equally,
I just hope one day,
Every man, woman and child,
Will be able to sit at the table of brotherhood
Together.

Jake Hale (12)
Devizes School, Devizes

My mum

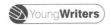

My mum makes it fun
She makes me laugh and chuckle.

When she's done the dishes
And fed the fishes
She rings her friends to say, 'Hey!'

When I'm feeling down
She picks me up and supports me in every way.

When she's put all the laundry away
She makes the best soup of the day.

When she sits to rest
She may not be at her best
But it's nice to see her be.

When she says, 'Goodnight'
I feel I almost might
Be as amazing as her one day!

So, let there be a boom, a wahay
Because I think my mum's the best
Hooray!

Louise Clements (13)
Devizes School, Devizes

Maybe Some Day

Maybe some day
People will think and consider others before they act.

Maybe some day
We will learn from the past and our mistakes.

Maybe some day
Everyone will get along and be equal.

Maybe some day.

Finn Burge (12)
Devizes School, Devizes

The World

Global warming, is so annoying
It only destroys the world
Something should be done

Bullies are mean, they aren't so keen
They destroy your dream
Something should be done

Killing an animal will only be emotional
For all the people around you
Something should be done

Littering will only lead to bickering
By the time you're caught
Something should be done

Don't do the crime
If you can't do the time
Something should be done

Stand up for your rights
Put up a fight
Something should be done!

Ricky Bhanot (13)
Devizes School, Devizes

A Tribute

This person
Helped other people,
When no one else would.
Picked them up when they were falling down,
They changed the world,
Just them, no one else,
That's what makes them special to me.

To be so faithful . . . in other people,
Incredible.

Thomas Jelves (11)
Devizes School, Devizes

Jason Robinson OBE

Stands at five foot eight
But weighs twelve stone eleven
He's made of muscle

When he plays rugby
He may sometimes play fullback
But mostly winger

He helped England win
Against Australia
Twenty-seventeen

Scored twenty-eight tries
For the England rugby team
The fifth most ever

By the Queen was given
MBE then OBE
Four years between them

Jason Robinson
I chose him as my idol
He is a legend.

Ben Poulton (13)
Devizes School, Devizes

Dream Poem

These our school leaders,
Which help us come first in groups
And compete in games.

Nelson Mandela,
He was loved by the people,
Whether black or white.

Mother Teresa,
Helped the others around her,
A mother to friends.

Martin Luther King,
He stood in front of a crowd
And told his mad dream.

Mahatma Gandhi,
He tried to make peace for all,
Spreading his strong words.

My inspirations,
Go to these great four people,
For their peace and love.

Regan Hodges (12)
Devizes School, Devizes

Pukka!

Jamie, oh, you inspire me!
Creating yummy food
Mine's good when I'm in the mood!

Slice, chop, dice
Salt, pepper, spice
Bake, fry and roast
Or just some toast!

Jamie, oh, you inspire me!
'Pukka!' you say
Restaurants we won't pay!

Spoon, knife, fork
Lamb, beef, pork
Sweet or sour
Even a pizza tower!

Cook then munch
To eat our lunch
After reading your books
I want to be a cook!

Saffron Russ (12)
Devizes School, Devizes

Inspiring Poem

This is for a baby that will never be born
This is for a baby that will never grow up
This is for a baby who will never cry a tear
This is for a baby that will never have a birthday party
This is for a baby that will never ride a bike
This is for a baby that will never go to school
This is for a baby that will never make friends
This is for a baby that will never have a first kiss
This is for a baby that will never be able to form a family
This is for an unborn baby that will always be loved.

Freddie Camacho & Amber Spanswick (13)
Devizes School, Devizes

I Have A Dream

As he once said in Washington DC
'I have a dream'
From that day on, we all knew he had a dream.

Day by day, month by month
We all take a step
That step we take, takes us so close
To where we need to be

Inspired you, inspired me
He joined the world together
Soon the time will come
For us to work in peace and harmony

As he once said in Washington DC
'I have a dream'

Stuck in our hearts
He is Martin Luther King

Let us walk forward together!
God bless you.

Kayleigh Sainsbury (13)
Devizes School, Devizes

The Path

We do not know what will happen in the future
All we can do is change now.

If we all do a small part it opens up the bigger picture
And the future becomes clearer.

There is a path
A long, hard path
But you want the right one
Which way do you go?

There's only one way to go forward.

Oscar Hall (14)
Devizes School, Devizes

Inspiration

It's what I'm doing now,
What I will be,
For the rest of my life,
It gives me hope
And helps me believe,
That I will do what I want to,
To become who I want to be,
I want to be a doctor,
A cardio-thoracic surgeon
And inspiration will help me get there,
I will believe,
I will be in those shoes one day
And that is the person I am,
I try to help everyone,
No matter how different they are,
I want to carry on doing that,
For the rest of my life,
That is the person I am
And aspire to be.

Stephanie Underwood (12)
Devizes School, Devizes

I Have A Dream

I have a dream
That everyone is treated equally
Black or white
Thin or fat
Tall or short
Everyone is unique in their own little way
Everyone has something special about them
Everyone has that twinkle in their eye
And everyone has a heart filled with love
Just waiting to be shared out.

Megan Gatty, Heidi Stockhill & Paige Rowlatt (13)
Devizes School, Devizes

I Have A Dream

I am not a star
I don't have much
But the guy who inspires me
I shout out his name
Travis Pastrana
Travis Pastrana
He is so swish
Pulling a whip
Blinding the crowd
With his awesome drift
And not forgetting his huge crib
From the 50in telly
To the big foam pit
I have a dream
To become like him
With all of the cars and wife
Travis Pastrana
Travis Pastrana
He is my king.

Josh Lewis (13)
Devizes School, Devizes

I Have A Dream

In my dream, I'm Robbie Keane,
The finest footballer you've ever seen,
Give me the ball and watch me go,
I really am the star of the show,
At White Hart Lane I'm number one,
I give the supporters so much fun
And when it comes to hitting the net,
There really is no surer bet,
So all in all, it must be seen,
The finest footballer, I'm Robbie Keane.

Kyran Marsh (11)
Devizes School, Devizes

The Heroes Of The Western Front

The officer shouts, 'A minute
'Til we go over the top.'
I'm glad I'm fighting for my country
Because I'm definitely scared.

The officer orders us
To fix bayonets
I'm glad I'm fighting for my country
Because I'm definitely scared.

The officer orders us to be ready
To go over the top
I'm glad I'm fighting for my country
Because I'm definitely scared.

The officer blows the whistle
To go over the top to meet the Fritz
I'm glad I'm fighting for my country
Because I'm definitely scared.

Then everything goes black . . .

Daniel Carpenter (12)
Devizes School, Devizes

My Mate - Pritika

When Pritika was one she made a bun
Turning two she was on her own to the loo
Then she turned three, she came to me
When she became four she could slam the door
Here comes number five and she gave me a high five
When she turned six she ate her first pick and mix
Then she became seven, she'd heard of Heaven
Became eight and became my mate
When she turned nine she made the day shine
Turned ten, she nicked my pen
When she became eleven, she went on a trip to Devon!

Kate Moore (14)
Devizes School, Devizes

War

It's terrible
It's bad
There are lives always being lost
Why? Why? Why?

Is there a world out there with peace across the land,
With beautiful fields?
But why is there war?
Why? Why? Why?

Good luck to our boys at war
To help us and all out there
But why fight?
Why? Why? Why?

Help each other with words
Words are powerful
Words are strong
So end the war with words
Words! Words! Words!

Jack Bramwell (13)
Devizes School, Devizes

I Have A Dream

I have a dream
A dream that the world stops getting slaughtered
By guns and knives,
A dream that people, any colour, are kind
And helpful to each other,
A dream that everyone could help in some way
To save the environment,
A dream where kids can roam freely
Without getting hurt or sexually assaulted,
A dream that the world can be a better place from now.

I have a dream, that was my dream.

Chris Burleton (14)
Devizes School, Devizes

Dreams

Everybody has different dreams about what life will bring them
Some people might dream about what they want to do
When they're older
Or just where they might be living or who they are with
In your lives, it's good to dream
Sometimes it gives you a taste of what life might just bring you
I have a dream, that one day life will bring everything I want
Like a journalist job, where I write lots of articles
Or maybe even a dental hygienist
I am very grateful for the life I have and what I've been given
I wouldn't swap it at all
I feel so sorry for the people in Africa
No food or drink, or even shelter
Some don't even go to school
To help them gain knowledge of the world around them
They have to walk miles to the nearest water tap
To get water for their families
I have a good life so we should be grateful for what God gave us.

Chloe Turnnidge (12)
Devizes School, Devizes

Emotions

Happiness is brilliant orange
It tastes like strawberries and cream
And smells like melted chocolate
It looks like Mr Happy from Mr Men
It feels like dancing the night away.

Fear is dark blue
It tastes like dead chicken
And smells like a roast dinner
It looks like the ghosts are coming
Fear sounds like a scream
It feels scary.

Hollie Anderson (11)
Devizes School, Devizes

I'm On The Road To Home

The leaves are falling from the trees
The snow is coming soon, don't you know
The leaves will soon be there again
I'm on the road to home

The sun will melt your heart
The wind will blow you back
The beaches will try and keep you there
I'm on the road to home

The leaves are here to stay
The snow has faded away
The tulips are blooming again
I'm on the road to home

The snow is falling like flour
The sun will soon melt the snowman
The sledges take me further
I'm on the road to home.

Jessica Dyton (14)
Devizes School, Devizes

The War

Every day could be their last
As their fight for survival takes a blast
Bullets ripping through the air
Bombs blow up, parents cry
The day feels like weeks
As scared soldiers can't sleep.

The terrorists succeed in their evil plan
Peace to the world is nowhere to be seen
The end is coming
But no one knows when
My dream is fiction
But this war is fact.

Ashley Beattie (14)
Devizes School, Devizes

Dreams

Dreams, we all have them,
To be a teacher or prime minister,
You may think that you can't reach them,
So don't change them, even for the better.

You have personal ones and global ones,
Like Gandhi, Mother Teresa, Mandela and King,
They were so dedicated to help us all
And never stopped trying.

Three of them ended up dead,
Mandela had to break the laws,
Gandhi got shot in the head,
But they died for a great cause.

You don't have to be famous to be helpers,
Everyone in your family has their roles,
Siblings, parents, teachers and tutors,
They all help us to reach our goals.

Toby Lock (14)
Devizes School, Devizes

My Dad

My dad, my dad
A scallywag as a lad

A lad, a lad
Always playing footie
Cos he's far from bad

Bad, bad
That definitely isn't my dad
Cos now he is footie mad

Footie, footie
As great as my dad can be
To forever inspire me.

Grant Bridewell (13)
Devizes School, Devizes

How I Wanna Be

H is for Hannah Montana
O is for over the hill
W is for winner, what I wanna be

I is for in it to win it

W is for when I grow up
A is for all the time
N is for Neyo
N is for nearly there
A lmost there

B is for the biggest
E is for the end and that's the end

I have a dream
And I will fight to get that dream
Also I have a dream
And a place to get that dream!

Kirstin Louise Baxter (12)
Devizes School, Devizes

Gran-Nan

Sherry, pop socks, morning TV,
Cancer three times, hot cups of tea,
Always by foot, never a car,
I love you, Gran-nan, for all that you are.

Family, friends, cats and dogs,
Spiders, horses, toads and frogs,
A heart of gold and in my heart,
I love you Gran-nan, for all that you are.

You look out for us, we look after you,
We are grateful for all that you do,
We love you, you're a total star,
We love you, Gran-nan, for all that you are!

Emily Smith (13)
Devizes School, Devizes

I Have A Dream

Every day is a fight for survival
They are doing this for you
The guns, your eardrums pop
The bombs, your arms get blown off . . .
They are doing this for you
The screams, as the guns fire once more
The fight for lives every second
They are doing this for you
Running with my soldiers
Seeing the fright in their eyes, terrified myself
Pieces of shrapnel flying by you
Not knowing who's going to get injured next
They are doing this for you
Seeing so many lives lost over nothing
I have a dream that one day this will end . . .
They are doing this for you.

Jenna Hitchcott (14)
Devizes School, Devizes

Lewis Hamilton

L et me go, I am
E xtreme, so let me go
W e are in the lead
I saw one
S chumacher fly past, fly past

H amilton, go, you really need to go, I
A m ready
M assa, just gone past
I have really got to go, so
L et me go
T est the wheels
O we my car, it
N early went too far.

Ben Cottrell (13)
Devizes School, Devizes

One Day . . .

One day,
Everyone in this world will have a home to go to,
One day,
Everyone will do their bit to make a greener world,
One day,
Everyone will have clean and fresh drinking water,
One day,
Everyone will have a good education,
One day,
There will be no malaria,
One day,
This world will have no CO_2 emissions,
One day,
There will be no recession,
One day,
We will have a peaceful world.

Megan Taylor (11)
Devizes School, Devizes

Tears

You're black, I'm white,
What's the problem?
There should be no fight.

I win, you lose,
What's the problem?
Don't be blue.

Please don't fight,
It is not right,
Come on guys, look on the bright side.

Life is here, don't be dull,
Life is to live,
To live to the full.

Lily May Elder (12)
Devizes School, Devizes

Independent Woman

This one lady,
She inspires me,
What she does in reality,
Is only a dream to me,
She sings what she feels,
What she feels is real,
She dances from the heart and expresses herself,
There's more to her than just fame and wealth,
She's brave and beautiful you see,
Things I can only wish to be,
The woman I'm talking about is Beyoncé Knowles,
She lightens up everybody's souls,
With her catchy tunes and shimmery hair,
You'll find fans of her everywhere,
I have a dream
To be everything she can be.

Beccy Smith (12)
Devizes School, Devizes

The Sea

He slithers up the sand,
Slowly, smoothly, swiftly,
He backs away hurriedly,
Turning into a great, noisy mountain.

He roars at small children,
Paddling in the shallows,
Slowly, smoothly, swiftly,
He takes all the world's troubles with him.

He brings with him many interesting things,
Shells, seaweed and starfish,
He provides a home for them
That many others in the world cannot have.

Chloe Stobbart (12)
Devizes School, Devizes

Frankie

Many people inspire me, but one sticks out
His name is Frankie, he doesn't like to pout
When I first met him, I used to stand and stare
But now I really like him and I don't care
He tries to make me jump, every once in a while
At this he's very good, but then, so am I

The reason he inspires me, is this
All the things that he would like, he works very hard
Just to get those things

When I am older, I want to work hard
So that I can do the things I want to
And hopefully be an inspiration to other people
Like if they want to be a sports star
They've got to train hard
And never give up to be the best they can.

Jack Wilson (13)
Devizes School, Devizes

I Have A Dream

I believe that all people should be treated with respect

H ave equal rights and a fair say
A ll of the people, black or white
V otes should count
E lections won fairly

A ll people should be treated with respect

D ifferent skin tones should not change our opinion of others
R ealise that black people are no different to white
E veryone should treat others the way they want to be treated
A ll people should be treated with respect
M y name is Nelson Mandela and I have a dream.

Emily Buller (12)
Devizes School, Devizes

I Have A Dream

I have a dream
That people will not
Shout at each other
And will not fight each other
They will sit and chat
To each other

I have a dream
That people will not
Be lazy and pollute the world
They will get on their bikes
And ride

That is my dream
And only you can make it come true

Thank you.

Kristian Scott (12)
Devizes School, Devizes

My Hopes For The Future

I think I can predict the future,
A life of dead-hard torture,

All humans will have flying cars,
Some living on Earth, some on Mars,

The animals will hardly be there,
Their population will be bare,

The sun and sky will disappear,
Forget the moon, it's never here,

The food on Earth will all have changed,
Dinner and tea are differently arranged,

To conclude; the world will be such a scare,
I'm just glad that I won't be there!

Matthew Ayliffe (12)
Devizes School, Devizes

To Every Victim

To every victim who is covered in fear,
This is for everyone whose cries you can't hear.

Letting people know can sometimes make it worse,
But that's the thing you should do first.

This is for every victim who can't open the door,
Always knowing that there is someone waiting for you,
But don't worry, there is something that you can do.

To every victim who gets punched in the head,
One more and you could be dead.

For the final stage, don't let it go on anymore,
As you could get very sore.

Bullies don't know the pain and fear,
Bullies don't know the cries and tears.

Raj Bhanot & Craig Burbidge (14)
Devizes School, Devizes

My Friend, Paul

(Written in memory of Lance Corporal Paul Upton)

Paul was a bloke,
Who blended into the crowd.
Paul was a man,
Who I looked up to.
Paul was a laugh,
Fair and compassionate.
At annual camp, he helped one and all,
My boots broke, so he gave me his.
To Afghanistan he went,
Fought for Queen and country.
He gave his life, so that we can all live without fear
I looked up to him, my hero,
My friend, Paul.

Joe Young (14)
Devizes School, Devizes

Me On My Bike

The sound of the engine
The power underneath me
Going so fast
I can hardly see
My heart beats faster
This bike I must master
I'm in my own world
Tearing across the field
Me and my motorbike
As one, need each other
Like the Earth needs the sun
Falling off is not a fear
I'm safe as I'm wearing all the right gear
Can I go faster still, before I go home?
I must get my thrill!

Dean Nield (12)
Devizes School, Devizes

Inspiration

I am inspired by my mum,
Who is very good at art.
I am inspired by my dad,
Who is very smart.
I am inspired by the RSPCA,
Who help animals in dismay.
I am inspired by animals themselves,
Who live their lives as they may.
I am inspired by many,
Who teach me every day.
I wish to be a forensic scientist,
Ever since I was young
And since I'm still at school,
My story has only just begun.

Jessie Coltart (12)
Devizes School, Devizes

Inspirational

I n life, people will try to hurt you, but never let them
hurt your heart
N ever look back and regret
S mile when you are most upset and angry
P eople who inspire me to do my best
I n time, people grow stronger and wiser
R oses are red, but violets are not you, so don't
Be something you're not
A t times you might feel sad, but look up at the sky and smile
T o try your best, even in the worst conditions
I n and out friends go, but you know who the true ones are
O pen up your heart to the ones who love you
N ot a lot of people know the real you
A lways believe in yourself, even when people don't believe in you
L ife is short, so make the most of it.

Rhianna Andrew (13)
Devizes School, Devizes

I Have A Dream

I have a dream
That people will not pollute the Earth
I have a dream
That people will not do drugs
Or anything that will hurt their bodies
I have a dream
That people will not hurt or kill other people
Because they feel like it or just for fun
I have a dream
That you will dream these same things
Just like I do
So don't be afraid to dream
I have a dream
That all people will be fair and kind.

Andrew Burleton (12)
Devizes School, Devizes

I Have A Dream

In my dream there will be no racism
Because I think everybody in the world should be equal.
Another thing I don't like is violence
I think if you don't like the person, walk away
And keep your life as happy as you want
And just forget about the person you hate.
Another thing which will not be in my dream, is war
Because there is violence and I do not like violence.
I have a dream that all people should have equal amounts of money
And there will not be poor people or rich people
There will be people all the same.
I think in my dream, there will be no abortion
Because all humans deserve to live
And babies deserve to have their first birthday
I have a dream!

Carl Ledbury (13)
Devizes School, Devizes

I Have A Dream

I n my dream team, these are the main players

H ope my dream comes true
A rsenal I will play for
V ictory will be ours
E xcept when we lose

A lmunia, the keeper

D iaby the midfielder
R obin Van Persie the striker
E duardo, back from injury
A nd gone straight back to injury, and
M e, myself, the midfielder.

Tommy Arkle (13)
Devizes School, Devizes

Family

My family have always inspired me,
They have always stuck by me,
They know me better than anyone,
I look up to my parents in a way I look at no other,
They have brought me up and kept me safe,
They have taught me what's wrong and what's right,
My brother and my sisters were there along the way too
And I have many happy memories that they created for me,
I don't think I ever said thank you properly,
But they deserve a thank you for all they have done for me
And all they have given me,
Thank you!

Livvy Moss (13)
Devizes School, Devizes

Summer

When summertime comes around,
All you want to do is shout aloud,
Whilst the little birds sing
And you think about the end of spring.
Summertime has arrived,
It makes you feel so alive,
To do so many exciting things,
It feels like you have magical wings.
To conquer mountains, sailing seas,
Marathon running and climbing up trees,
The sun is my fuel, that lifts me throughout the day,
So I'll just be sad when the sun goes away!

Louise Pfeil (13)
Devizes School, Devizes

The Soldier

A soldier is brave
A soldier will fight
A soldier will keep us safe in the night
A soldier will save our lives
A soldier is honest, courageous and true
A soldier gives his life to save me and you
A soldier will keep freedom alive
A soldier will stop the bombs of tomorrow
A soldier will wait for a letter from home
A soldier will not moan
A soldier, in my eyes, is a hero.

Fraser Nash (11)
Devizes School, Devizes

My Inspirations

Best friends are your inspirations
They teach you that not everything is bad
They teach you to laugh, play and have fun
They listen and comfort
But the best thing about my best friends
Is that they have taught me to follow my dreams
And to stand for what I believe in
They say that one day I will fulfil my dreams
But my dream is now
My dream is that I have friends as good as them
Friends that I will remember forever.

Kayleigh Millar (12)
Devizes School, Devizes

There Will Be One Day . . .

There will be one day
When animal cruelty will be stopped forever.

There will be one day
When animals will no longer have to chew on a tether.

And one day
All animals will never be left outside in all weather.

There will be one day
When no innocent animal will be sold for meat.

There will be one day
When all animals can relax while they eat.

And one day
All animals will not break in a sweat and feel the heat.

There will be one day
When all animals deserve to enjoy life and have fun.

There will be one day
When all animals can proudly shout out that they have won.

And one day
All animals can escape testing labs then pay them back
for what they have done.

There will be one day
When all animals will have hope and their strength will show.

There will be one day
When all animals will feel better and never get down that low.

And one day
All animals will never feel tortured again but simply just glow.

There will be one final day
When all animal cruelty will be stopped forever
And the cruelty will finally end.

Charlotte Vockins (12)
Highworth Warneford School, Swindon

Stop Child Abuse

Children rely on you to look after them
Not just to live in a play pen
Children are little precious things
Who like to rhyme and sing.

Children don't ask to be born
Just let them see the dawn
Their life is in your hands
Let them feel the freedom of the lands.

Children are small, cute and tiny
Don't hurt them even if they are whining
They have faith in you
Can you have faith in them too?

They can't look after themselves
They need your help
They aren't that old
Don't let them be cold.

Children need a mum and dad
Not just to be sat there, being sad
Children suffer in silence
With their mum and dad being violent.

Children need some role models
Not just to be left to toddle
They need some help
Not left to yelp.

Children can't just be pushed into a corner
You don't have the right to push them, because you're taller
Someone needs to tell you how to look after your children
You can't just push them about
You need to listen to me
Stop! Stop! Stop!

Tiana Francis (12)
Highworth Warneford School, Swindon

Homework

The day that I never have homework,
Is a day that I look forward to,
But I know it won't come,
Until I'm twenty-one
And finished both college and school.

The person who sets homework is evil,
An amazing example of bad,
For he puts children through pain,
Just to earn fame,
Of being stricter than anyone's dad.

There are some who could stop this,
The people in power can,
The government could,
The government should,
But they have a scheming plan.

The people of tomorrow,
Will be like robots in due time,
Cos if they do homework now,
Then they will not row,
No, they will never step out of line.

And now that I have unveiled this,
Us school kids should stand and fight,
Against the toffs
And against the boffs,
Who think that homework is right.

So, let us all stand together
And make sure that the wrongs are now right,
For homework is gone,
Put your best clothes on,
Cos we're going on a party night!

Bradley Caton-Garrett (13)
Highworth Warneford School, Swindon

Future, Present And Past

When I'm older, I would like to be an architect or vet,
But I'll have to work hard, because I'm not there yet.
I would like to have a family and some animals too,
A dog, some chickens and a whole lot from the zoo.
I would like to go to Africa and help the poor,
Meet one or two families, maybe four.
I want to help slow down global warming and so should you,
Because you know that it is affecting your future too.

So, that's what I want to do when I'm older, but what about now?
I could do all sorts of things, even eat a whole cow!
I want to become a really good swimmer, so I can win lots of races,
I want to see all sorts of things and go to all sorts of places.
I'd like to do something for charity and raise lots of money,
I could run a marathon, eat a worm, or do something funny.
There are lots of things I can learn, play, do and enjoy,
But one thing I really want to do, is meet Fall Out Boy!

When I was young, I did all sorts of things,
Played all sorts of games and pretended I had wings!
I went to places like Ireland, Scotland and Wales,
I would be interested in little things, like slugs and snails!
I went to Disneyland, which was really magical,
Nothing really bad happened to me, nothing tragical!

So, that's what I did when I was younger
And what I want to do now,
What I want to do when I'm older and when and how.
All sorts of things will happen, good and bad,
But one thing I know is that I hope I don't go mad!

Emma Hazell (13)
Highworth Warneford School, Swindon

No More School

I have a dream

I have a dream
That one day there will be no more school rushes in the morning.

I have a dream
I have a dream
That no more little kids will wake up early.

I have a dream

I have a dream
That one day children will be able to do
What they want at the weekend.

I have a dream

I have a dream
That one day there will be no such thing as detention.

I have a dream

I have a dream
That one day teachers will get another job
And never have to shout at bad children.

I have a dream

I have a dream
That one day children can live their dreams
Before going through their idea of Hell.

I have a dream.

Matthew Crouch (12)
Highworth Warneford School, Swindon

Me, The Superhero

When I grow up, I want to be a superhero,
Not a mere little zero,
Gravity will be my name,
To beat up bad guys will be my aim.

I want to drive nice cars
And have superpowers,
Be able to fly
And pick up towers.

I want X-ray vision,
Be super-strong,
Go on secret missions
And be friends with King Kong.

The Joker is no match for me,
Before he smiles,
On the floor he shall be.

Lex Luther is a bald man,
That's because I nicked his hair
And hit him with a pan.

Dr Octopus has eight legs,
But I cut them off
And hit him on the head.

Thank you for listening to what I want to be,
Maybe you could be a superhero with me?

Joseph Birch (13)
Highworth Warneford School, Swindon

Poverty Poem

I have a dream to stop poverty,
I see the people on the streets, sitting in doorways, as I walk past,
I see the people on the streets, begging for change, as I walk past,
I see the people who are ill, waiting for death to walk past,
I see the people on the streets, thinking, *why must I have left?*
I have a dream to stop seeing poverty.

I smell the people stinking of pee, as I walk past,
I smell the people thinking of the smell of sweet food,
as I walk past,
I smell the people thinking, *I'm so hungry,* as I walk past,
I smell the people smelling of fish, as I walk past,
I have a dream to stop smelling poverty.

I see my dream becoming real,
I see the people in warm beds, as I help them get a home,
I see the people eating food, as I help give them food,
I see the people think, *I'm glad I left,* as I am their friend,
I see my dream becoming real.

I smell my dream becoming real,
I smell the people stinking of cleanliness, as I wash them,
I smell the people thinking of the smell of sweet food,
as it's placed before them,
I smell them think, *I'm so full!* as I take the empty plate from them,
I smell my dream becoming real,
I see my dream, I smell it - it's real.

Talitha Cogan-Stevens (12)
Highworth Warneford School, Swindon

I Have A Dream

I have a dream
There was no pollution
That there was no civil war
That all the bad would stop
And the poor could grow their crops!

I wish
There would be peace
That there would be no abuse
People would be filled
With love and care.

So soon
The animals could be treated with kindness
That there was no such thing as abandonment.

I have a dream
The world is as safe as can be.

I wish that there was a cure
To all the badness in the world.

There's more to life than just money
More to life than toys
It's all about what you can do.

I have a dream for you.

Alice Barnfield (11)
Highworth Warneford School, Swindon

I Have A Dream . . .

I have a dream
Of eating cream
So delicious and very clean
No lumps and not too runny
Mmm . . . that's just yummy!

Tarek Ishty (13)
Highworth Warneford School, Swindon

An Important Dream

I have a dream
That one day poverty will end,
I have a dream
The world united as a friend.

Today, there is poverty
Tomorrow there is no more,
A window in the course of history,
Another step, an open door.

I am going to stop the poverty
Together we will fight,
United as a nation
My dream will take flight.

With the help of my friends
Today, not tomorrow,
We can fight this dreadful thing
We will stop the sorrow.

I have a dream
To keep this challenge alive,
This is an important dream
So, for this I will strive.

Phoebe Smith (12)
Highworth Warneford School, Swindon

I Have A Dream

Time is changing, we haven't got long,
This is a rhyme and not as song.
Animals are struggling, they just can't bear,
They don't have long - don't pretend you don't care.

We are acting like cannibals,
The whales just might die.
Have a heart for these helpless animals,
Vegetation is of short supply.

The ice caps are melting,
The penguins are about to go.
Far, far away from all their food,
Warmth and snow.

Let's all work together,
To make this world a better place.
Reuse, reduce, recycle,
Let's try and save the race.

By me writing this poem,
I hope I've made a point.
My dream is that in the future,
We will be recycling at the joint.

Charlotte Berry (12)
Highworth Warneford School, Swindon

I Have A Dream

Life on a peaceful Yorkshire farm,
Galloping over rolling hills of grass,
The sun setting over the purple moors,
Cockerel alarm clocks waking you up,
Birds cheeping in the morning, singing to each other,
Cows, sheep and horses grazing in the fields,
I lay in the fields of corn, feeling the wind across my face,
I am living the dream.

Diving under the cool water,
A rush of adrenaline washing over my body,
I burst through the top of the pool,
I use my strong, powerful arms to glide through the water,
I hit the wall at the end,
Was I fast enough? I look up at the board,
My time is coming up,
It feels like time has slowed down,
One minute and twelve seconds . . . I've won!
I jump out of the water, ready to receive my gold medal,
I stand on the podium waving to the world,
I set a new world record,
I am living the dream.

Lizzie Snell (12)
Highworth Warneford School, Swindon

I Have A Dream

I have a dream
For the world to gleam
And not be so dull and mean!

To keep it safe
You have to have faith
It's just really sad
Everyone thinks it's so bad!

I have a dream
For the world to be
So beautiful, bubbly and bright
Yes, it's scary
But we could help like a little fairy!

Why is it much trouble?
It's all a big bubble
We truly can make a change!

I have a dream
For everything not to seem
So terrible, cruel and dark!

I have a dream . . .

Ella Watkins (12)
Highworth Warneford School, Swindon

I Have A Dream

I shall search for the truth.
Every tiny speck will be important.
I shall study the motes of blood,
The broken bones,
The angry bruises
From the head to the foot.

I shall make sure justice is done.
The criminal will pay.
As I comb for clues and seemingly insignificant details,
Every thread,
Every strand
Will speak to me.

And I will find the villain.

I shall show patience and skill.
Science will be my friend.
And the weak,
The vulnerable,
The innocent
Shall find a friend in me.

Charlie Ward (12)
Highworth Warneford School, Swindon

The Olympics

I have a dream
That one day I will go to the Olympics
Not for swimming,
I just sink,
Not for running,
I'm way too slow,
Not for diving,
Because I stink,
Maybe I won't go to the Olympics after all!

Toby Dibble (13)
Highworth Warneford School, Swindon

Take Me Away

Take me away,
To a place with peace and a calm world.
Take me away,
Where there is no war, no falling out and no fighting.
Take me away,
To a Neverland, where everything is perfect
Apart from the souls within us are relaxed,
That are willing to do what it takes for someone sad to turn happy,
Who will never give up on their dreams.
Take me away,
Somewhere where people reach their goals
And achieve their highest success.
Take me away,
To a place where people take responsibility for their actions
And who do not take it out on someone innocent.
Take me away,
To a place where someone is proud of their culture
And someone who is not ashamed
As to what country they come from.
Take me away.

Layla Rich (12)
Highworth Warneford School, Swindon

One Day I Shall Do . . .

Skydiving
Rock climbing
Have an easy life
Get rich
Ride in a helicopter
Get good at art
And at darts
So
Now you know what I want to do!

Rosesh Rai (12)
Highworth Warneford School, Swindon

Travel The World

I have a dream,
One day I will travel the world,
To go up mountains
And swim the seas,
To ride through the deserts,
To shiver in the Arctic
And clamber up volcanoes.

I hope that you will admire,
My genuine desire,
To travel widely and see what I can,
Cos I have but a short lifespan.

My dream is ever constant,
To roam freely where I will,
To take in natural wonders
And a lot of bright lights too.

I have a dream,
Very ambitious, even optimistic,
Or so it would seem!

Alex Daniels (12)
Highworth Warneford School, Swindon

Stop Our Bully

I have a dream that for bullying to be stopped fully
I have a dream that even you can get rid of your bully

From seeing children suffer and cry
To making those gleaming eyes dry

I have a dream that children will not be hit
By older or younger people, for doing nothing wrong

I will stop children, or maybe even adults
Being called horrid remarks

I shall stop bullies from getting away with it
And I will stop it forever

I know and I'm sure you do too
Think that bullies are nothing but a piece of stupid goo

I want all of us to stand here today and to think
Stop bullying forever, but I need your help!

We have this dream
Let's make it reality!

Jamie Carter (13)
Highworth Warneford School, Swindon

A Dream Is A Dream

A dream is a dream
S o I have a dream
T o be known in history
R adiation won't stop me
O n Mars I will land
N o meteor will stop me, nor space junk
A dream is a dream
U nder the control of my heart I will not fail
T o be triumphant, to be known in history.

Alex Sly (11)
Highworth Warneford School, Swindon

Winning

Winning this competition,
Is a very grand idea,
Winning this competition,
Would make me laugh and cheer!

Winning this competition,
Would be very grand indeed,
Winning this competition,
I would surely take the lead.

Winning this competition,
Would be very great for me,
Winning this competition,
Would make me dance with glee!

Winning this competition,
Would make me very proud,
Winning this competition,
Would make me shout out loud!

Winning this competition.

Thomas Hipkin (12)
Highworth Warneford School, Swindon

Falling Ice

Did you know that there is a place
Where the deserted land speaks to the world?
A place that has the class of the stars,
A place where the most secretive creatures dwell,
A place that is falling, crumbling, dying.

Did you know that there is a place
That is the victim of destruction?
A place where the ice sparkles,
A place where the sights are unbelievable,
A place that is beauty, wonder, joy.

Did you know that there is a place
Where the sky lights up on special nights?
A place that only few have experienced,
A place that can challenge the toughest of people,
A place that brings amazement and love,
But it has not long to live.

Did you know there is a place?

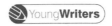

Chandni Mistry (13)
Highworth Warneford School, Swindon

I Have A Dream

I have a dream
A dream that everyone is treated the same
Think of a world where people can walk down the street
Without worrying about being harmed or mugged
Think about it, that's what it should be like
All we need is for people to agree on making a decision.

I have a dream
A dream and that dream is a world
With *no* wars and *no* poverty and *no* drugs.

I have a dream
That in this world we can accept people for who they are
And not judge people by the colour of their skin or eyes
People will never create a perfect world
But we can do things, like all the countries respect international laws
With all of these little changes
We could make the world a very different place for the future.

Alastair Woodhead (12)
Highworth Warneford School, Swindon

Teenage Knife Crime

I believe we can stop teenage knife crime
I believe it's the right time
To stop the sorrow on people's faces
To made the streets welcome places

I believe we can stop the knives being sold
Without the parents being told
To stop the teenagers from doing this crime
I believe we need to give them a warning sign

I believe carrying a knife is not cool
Definitely after you have seen a blood pool
We can stop this, I know we will
I believe we can win, ten-nil

We will make the streets a happy place
I believe we can stop the sorrow on people's faces
I believe it's the right time
It's my dream to stop knife crime.

Rebecca Storey (12)
Highworth Warneford School, Swindon

My Dream

I have a dream that the world will be a peaceful place,
People won't be made fun of because of their race,
There will be no bloodshed or war
And no one will be too rich or too poor,
There will be no theft or crime
And no one will die before his or her time.
I have a dream that the world will be fair,
With no animals becoming extinct or rare,
There will be no hunger or thirst
And people will think of others first,
There will be no murder or assassinations
And no more war between the nations.

Harry Colderick (13)
Highworth Warneford School, Swindon

A Girl Can Dream

When I wish upon a star
And when I dream at night,
I think about those people,
That weren't given their rights.

Like the racism in the past
And the kindness in the present,
The change in the world,
Has made life so pleasant!
People are counted equal
And not judged by their skin,
Black and white can now have fun,
Because of the friends they've been!

Martin Luther King,
Would be so very proud!
Because the black and white,
Are now part of the same crowd!

Bethany Erin Stevens (12)
Highworth Warneford School, Swindon

My Dream

My dreams would be
To do well in my GCSEs,
To become a successful vet
And help many species of animals.

I'll choose my choices carefully,
The options I would enjoy,
I'd try different experiences,
Even if the risk is high.

I would try my hardest at everything,
Even if to fail,
But most of all I'd smile at every stage
Every day a new page.

Amy Linfield (13)
Highworth Warneford School, Swindon

My Dream

When I'm older, I'll cut up the dead,
I'll start with their feet and end with their head,
For the cops and the bill, I will slave,
Many people I will save.

I'll get home around eight and eat a nice tea,
Then sit by the telly, my kids, wife and me,
I'll get to bed early and rest my tired head,
Knowing that I've got a long day ahead.

At around six, I'll get out of bed
And go to work to examine the dead,
I'll do some post mortems and solve a crime,
Then I'll get home and have a big glass of wine.

This is a dream and I'll follow it through,
It is possible,
I'll show you!

Geoffrey William Maycock (13)
Highworth Warneford School, Swindon

I Have A Dream

I have a dream
That one day police will not be needed to patrol the streets
Because they will be free of crime and violence.

I have a dream
That we will have a crime-free world
Where everyone can be friends with each other.

I have a dream
That the RSPCA will not need to do their job
Because animal cruelty will no longer happen.

I have a dream
That all pets will be treated fairly and like part of the family
There will be no cruelty to animals.

Jamie Smith (12)
Highworth Warneford School, Swindon

I Need To Finish This Poem

I wish I could write a poem,
So that I can show 'em,
That I can rhyme,
Any day, any time,
I want to write a poem.

I need to write a poem,
So I can get a good job and show 'em,
That I can get an A
Any time, any day,
I want to write a poem.

I need to finish this poem,
So I can pass English and show 'em,
My poem is good enough,
To beat a poem that is good enough,
Hey, look! I've finished the poem!

Sarah Collyer (12)
Highworth Warneford School, Swindon

One Day

I wish that one day everyone would
Live in harmony with each other,
There will be no wars, no dictators or tyrants,
No evil, no living in fear.

I wish that every child would be bubbling with happiness,
People will care for each other, help each other,
No matter what colour, creed or religion,
Adorable animals will no longer be abandoned or ill-treated.

I wish that everyone will love, care and smile,
No more darkness, dirtiness or coldness,
But the sun will shine everywhere,
Warming our homes and glowing from within our hearts,
I hope that one day this will come true.

Laura Garnett (11)
Highworth Warneford School, Swindon

This Is My Dream

This is my dream
That one day I'll be on the stage,
Drums and me
The crash of the cymbal
The boom of the bass
The stream of sweat
Running down my face
The roar of the crowd
The crack of the snare
The vibration from the loudspeakers
Pounding through my hair
This is my future
Not my dream
I can achieve it
Watch and see!

Luke Townsend (12)
Highworth Warneford School, Swindon

I Have A Dream . . .

My dream is for the world to be safe
A place where you could walk past a stranger
And not have to be scared
To know you can trust anyone.

My dream is of a place where I feel safe
I'd love not to worry about anything
No wars, pain or sadness.

My dream is of a place of peace
Somewhere that *all* animals are treated
With the love and care they deserve.

My dream is for no cruelty
Always happy faces, never sad
No mean comments or hurtful words.

Alexandra McKay (12)
Highworth Warneford School, Swindon

I Have A Dream

I have a dream to be a cat,
Killing mice and be allowed to sleep all day,
I really don't want to be a bat,
In the sun I will lay.

My fur will be orange and white,
Stalk my prey and then I pounce,
I will have a very strong bite,
I will like to eat some mice,
I have a dream to be a cat.

When I climb trees, I can see far and wide,
At least now I can run from dogs,
I can catch mice, because I can hide,
Then when I am tired, I will go to sleep on a log,
I have a dream to be a cat.

Tim Hill (11)
Highworth Warneford School, Swindon

I Have A Dream

I have a dream to stop poverty

H elp adults, help children to have enough food
A nd that everyone has a happy life
V ery few people have enough money to survive
E veryone deserves a chance

A lso that children in poor countries have a family to grow up with

D ream I do, of a world that is poverty-free
R ight, right, right
E veryone has a right
A dream is a dream
M y dream will come true

I have a dream to stop poverty!

Libby Hale (12)
Highworth Warneford School, Swindon

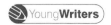

The Adrenalin Rush

Precision and accuracy are needed here,
To guide your horse for he does not fear,
Confidence and praise to give your horse,
The skill and power to complete the course.

Pounding hooves hit the ground,
Skilfully tackled up the mound,
Ears back, body tense,
Just enough energy to clear the fence.

Now gently, I ask his stride to spread,
He takes my word and raises his head,
Preparation to get here, might have been mean,
But now it's all over, we finished as a team.

Nicole Emms (13)
Highworth Warneford School, Swindon

One Day The World

One day the world will live in peace
And all will see the light
The endless wars will end at last
And hearts will shine bright.

One day the world will see
There is more to life than wealth
Some are left to starve and die
While we're in perfect health.

There *will* be a day
When all will leave the dull, dusk, dark
Live where they are loved and wanted
Today, reality is stark!

Ceara Coveney (11)
Highworth Warneford School, Swindon

I Have A Dream . . .

Are you happy to call this world your own creation?
Is this an equal world?
A world of justice and freedom?
No, it is not.
This is a world of shame,
A world where people are judged by the colour of their skin
And not for the kindness of their character or a true heart.
This is a crooked place, but crooked places can be made straight
And this world of injustice and imprisonment can and will be changed.
I had a dream the world would be a place where there is no
more hunger, war or suffering,
The world I would like to see, a place where no one is lost,
A world where no one cries, crying at all is not allowed.
In the dream I dreamed, no one is ever wronged or looked down upon.
It is a dream of freedom where all people are treated as an equal race.
We will not be satisfied until freedom rains from the heavens
above like water
And mends the wounds and scars civilisation has left on our brothers
And breaks the dams that separate black people from white people.
I had a dream that blacks and whites could sit together at the table
of brotherhood
And we will only then be satisfied.
When as brothers and sisters we can hold hands and sing
We will be satisfied,
And when this happens, our long journey will be over at last
And the world can live as one.
Then, and only then we will be satisfied,
When the world can live as one.

Chloe Frances Thomas (13)
Humphry Davy School, Penzance

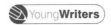

I Have A Dream

I don't have a dream
Of good or bad,
I just have a dream
Of life's injustices.

I see devils
Whipping the innocent as slaves
And the guilty running free
Among the hills and valleys.

I have a nightmare
Of no freedom,
Or justice,
Just Hell.

I see murderers and villains
As MPs and kings,
But only the non-forgiven
Criminals.

Monsters and demons
Roaming our streets
And killing our loved ones,
I have a nightmare.

I don't have a dream
Of good or bad,
I just have a nightmare
Of life's injustices.

I am not asleep.

George Somers (13)
Humphry Davy School, Penzance

ITV Was Born For Formula One

ITV is the true place for Formula One
Not BBC they have loads
ITV has intervals so you can go to the toilet
BBC does not so what is the point?

ITV was born for Formula One
So why have a change
Keep it the same
That is my dream.

Formula One won't be the same again
If you need a cuppa
You can't go if Formula One is on BBC
You would probably miss the best bit.

ITV was born for Formula One
So why have a change?
Keep it the same
That is my dream.

It could haunt us forever
If it's on the BBC
Formula One would probably go out of business
So to save Formula One
Put it back on ITV.

Tomas Newman (11)
Humphry Davy School, Penzance

A Dead Man's Dream

The sand in the hourglass is running low,
I came through thunder and lightning with the rain and the snow,
To find you away on this single bed, a sight for sore eyes but to kill.

So get off your low, let's dance like we used to,
And there's a light in the distance waiting for me, I will wait for you,
So get off your low, let's kiss like we used to.

Jack Kelly-Granger (12)
Humphry Davy School, Penzance

I Had A Dream

I have a dream
People will stop abuse
To others or creatures
Tears are disguised

I have a dream
People will stop hating each other
The leaking loneliness
Life must change
Let loneliness fade

Freedom will pass
Over the houses
Over rivers
Over oceans
Over land
Upon soft sands
Over the stones
Over skin and bones

The lonely lives
Let it help
The cloak of darkness disappear.

Michael Harvey (13)
Humphry Davy School, Penzance

I Have A Dream

I dream we would be free
And sit and have a cup of tea
The wars would finally end
And show people peace was around the bend

I wish people would stop the hate
And get along quite nicely
And have a good old skate
If you fall you would land lightly.

Luke Knight
Humphry Davy School, Penzance

Peace To All!

I have dreamt of a world of peace,
That love will never decrease.
I dream that we shall carry on
Living without any fear.

I dream that bullies would be extinct
And criminals as well.
I dream that no one would steal or cheat
Or lock people in cells.

I dream that smoking shall too be extinct,
The horrible smell of tobacco and smoke.
It looks foul, smells foul
And it's enough to make you choke!

I dream that wars will never begin
And no one will use guns.
I dream that no one will swear but they
Will join hands and dance in the sun.

So that's my dream,
What's yours?

Megan Hunter (12)
Humphry Davy School, Penzance

Dreams

The moon is the keyhole to a dream,
It locks so many in; it reads them one by one.
It then guides them to sleepyheads like a stream,
Cool, blessed water.
They can spark imagination,
They can bring freedom,
They are true magic in their own right.
They lead your life into a shoelace,
Knots and dirt, neat and tidy,
But a dream can stop injustice and bring peace.

Bronwyn Hocking (12)
Humphry Davy School, Penzance

A Robber Stole My Bacon

A robber came in to steal my bacon
He stole me radio that was Jamaican
When he'd awakened
He was forsaken
He forgot to steal me bacon
When I awakened
I was shaken
Me bacon had been taken
I was mistaken
It was me dog's bacon
So I became unshaken
When I reawakened
I saw me bacon
Dangling from me ceiling
I jumped to grab it
I fell down squealing
It was mouldy
It wasn't appealing.

James Goodwin (12)
Humphry Davy School, Penzance

I Have A Dream

I have a dream that all of life's problems will be gone!
I have a dream that there will be no war, no fighting, just peace!
I have a dream that there will be no illness!
I have a dream there will be no sadness, only happiness!
Together we can make this dream a reality!
If we join hands, no matter what skin colour you are
Or what country you are from!
Together we will make this dream a reality,
But only together can we make this dream a reality!

Chris Whatley (13)
Humphry Davy School, Penzance

What If I Could . . .

What if I could stop poverty?
What if I could stop extinction?
What if I could stop death?

We could if we tried.

What if I could stop war?
What if I could stop abuse?
What if I could stop deadly diseases?

We could if we tried.

What if I could stop murder?
What if I could stop racism?
What if I could stop judgement?

We could if we tried,
So stop your tears,
As there is a solution,
To the trouble we have caused.

Alicia Davey (12)
Humphry Davy School, Penzance

Grow Up World

I have a dream
A dream for the world to grow up
Grow up world
Families torturing children
Wars over nothing
Grow up world
Murders over money problems
Stabbing people over the colour of their skin
Grow up world.

Albert Tomlinson (11)
Humphry Davy School, Penzance

I Have A Dream About Children

I have a dream that children will
Live in peace, and that the amount of
Abuse will be decreased.

I have a dream that children will
Play outside, and not be trapped inside.
I have a dream that kids could be happy
And not get angry and snappy.

I have a dream that children will have
Essentials, and go to school to achieve their
Potentials.

I have a dream that children won't
Be left at home, but be in the garden
With parents that enjoy gnomes.

Do you have a dream?

Jomary Baemedi (11)
Humphry Davy School, Penzance

War And Peace Can Be The Same

War and peace can be the same,
Young men dying screaming its name.
War!
Smoke and fire engulf his face,
That's what happens in this blasted place.
The blue water stained red
From the man that lay in his resting bed.
War!
This is how he tells the tale
Because he's the one who made the bail.
War!
As he closed his eyes for the last time,
We know it's not him who did the crime.
It's war!

Daniel Palmer (12)
Humphry Davy School, Penzance

Food And Drink

I have a dream
That children will never starve
That parents will buy more food for the poor and hungry
If you do then you are caring
And look after your children by buying healthy and nutritious food
As well as buying sweets, chocolate and sugar.

I have a dream
That people will not buy Coke
And will stop using the Africans' water supply by buying it
It will make you guilty
It is unhygienic
My dream will hopefully come true.

This food and drink version
Of I had a dream.

Jack Round (12)
Humphry Davy School, Penzance

There Once Was A Dream

There once was a dream,
A dream to change the world,
To free us from war and poverty.

There once was a dream,
A dream to show peace,
To stop murder, hatred and racism.

There once was a dream,
A dream of a clean environment,
To stop pollution to our brains and to our world.

There once was a dream,
A dream that no longer exists,
That has been lost under our messy, confused world.

There once was a dream!

Harry Stevens (13)
Humphry Davy School, Penzance

Stop War, Make Peace

Everybody's dying,
Dying every minute,
Is this what you want?

Why do you like war?
Oh, so you don't like war?
Then why have a war?

Why don't you change war to peace
Because everyone loves peace
And peace is better than war.

Stop war, make peace,
Stop war, make peace,
Stop war, make peace,
Stop war, make peace.

Adam Paterson (11)
Humphry Davy School, Penzance

The Poem Of Peace

I have a dream
A dream of peace
And in the war
Everyone did not fight
But instead they became friends.

I have a dream
A dream that when I have children
Random people do not shout at them
When they're in the way.

I have a dream
A dream that when I die
I will want to rest in peace
So my children know I was happy.

Josh Round (12)
Humphry Davy School, Penzance

The Man Who Never Walked

I saw the man who never walked
My neighbour rang him and he always talked
I saw him stealing and he got caught
I never thought he got taught.

I saw the man who never walked
My neighbour saw him and he never talked
I saw him wheeling round the street
Listening to a wicked beat.

If I ever see him again
I don't know his name so I will call him Ben
If I ever go to the park
I think he'll have to leave before dark.

Bradley Gibson (11)
Humphry Davy School, Penzance

Smoking Kills

There are people on the streets
Getting cancer every week
You might as well stop
You'll get a longer life
To do your job.

Keep this in mind
It may change your life

Smoking kills.

Lukas Moticieus (12)
Humphry Davy School, Penzance

I Have A Dream

I have a dream that one day people will be free
I have a dream that there will be no poverty
I have a dream that we will look after our planet
I have a dream that there will be no war
I have a dream that we will have no need to kill
I have a dream that some day we will live together
I have a dream that we will not need help to realise
what's going on in the world.

Jessica Richards (13)
Humphry Davy School, Penzance

I Have A Dream

One person wanted to change the world
One person said a speech
One person changed the world for the better
One person knew the better for us
So just think of that dream when it becomes true
Because I will be free because that is my dream.

Tom King (13)
Humphry Davy School, Penzance

I Have A Dream

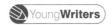

I have a dream,
I have a dream to ride my bike with no handlebars,
I have a dream to jump on moving cars,
I have a dream that people won't die,
I have a dream that people will be honest and won't lie.

Jake Baldwin (13)
Humphry Davy School, Penzance

I Have A Dream

I dream that all of the people were treated the same.
I wish that all of the people were helping each other in need.
I dream that all of the people were welcomed to other countries.
I wish that all of the countries were friends with each other.
I dream that Earth was a friendly place to live.

Igor Tsizdan (12)
Humphry Davy School, Penzance

Wild Peace - Haiku Against Deforestation

I wish for nature
To grow in grace, undisturbed,
And flourish in peace.

Sophie Curnow (12)
Humphry Davy School, Penzance

Dreams

I am a footballer,
I get paid quite a lot,
I have a big game coming up,
Maybe you could come and watch.

Two minutes until kick off,
I am very scared
Because we are playing
The roughest team out there.

It has all gone black!
I cannot see a thing!
Am I dead?
Is this Heaven I'm in?

Wait!
I can see!
I am in a room!
There is someone there, looking at me!

I know who this is!
It's my manager!
Who's that standing next to him?
It looks like a doctor!

I have now found out!
That is, what happened to me.
The doctor saved my life!
I am so lucky!

But the sad thing is,
This is no lie,
That I get paid more for playing a game
Than he does for saving lives!

This should be changed!
It's just not right!

Katy Bowyer (11)
Penrice Community College, St Austell

Votes

It was time again.
My brother walked towards the box.
I felt the urge to walk up and submit,
But I knew I couldn't.

This should change.
Children should vote.
They have as much right as the men.

Oh, I'm running out of patience!
He greeted me as he came back.
Little did he know that he, with all his great ideas,
Was to be the next president!

Who voted for him so much that he won?
Well, let's just say the closest person he has
To an only sibling!

Hayley Taylor (12)
Penrice Community College, St Austell

If Everyone Had The Same Vision?

If everyone had the same vision,
Crime would no longer be,
If everyone had the same vision,
We would live in a world of empathy.

If everyone had the same vision,
The world would be at peace,
If everyone had the same vision,
War would forever cease.

If everyone had the same vision,
No one would rebel,
If everyone had the same vision,
No one would go to hell.

Shannon Babb (12)
Plymouth High School for Girls, Plymouth

Will You Know Of Love?

Eyes, so blank, clear like glass,
People stop, stare, pass,
Beating sun, like sound of bass,
Will you know of love?

Why do tears roll down your face?
Why do you seem so out of place?
Judged by fear, by wealth, by race,
Will you know of love?

Sweltering in the brightest light,
Cold, hard floor in dead of night,
Survival is the toughest fight,
Will you know of love?

Give them hope, give them love,
Help them, and then rise above,
This terrible fate, like the peaceful dove,
Then you will know of love.

Hope Lucas (13)
Plymouth High School for Girls, Plymouth

My Flower

The beauty of a simple flower,
Always gentle and never sour.

Flying birds with fluttering wings,
Listen as the hummingbird sings.

Flowing rivers and flat, calm lakes,
Tremble as the monster wakes.

Digging holes and cutting trees,
Killing rabbits and squashing bees.

So all I ask, with all my heart,
Is for my flower to never depart.

Lerryn Warren (12)
Plymouth High School for Girls, Plymouth

I Do

I lay on the grass,
And think of the mass
Of stars above me.

I think of the sea
And the fish to be,
That lay on the mushy sand.

As I think of the grand,
That lay on the sand,
With the warmth above and below them.

I walk through the den,
That was made by him,
I think he was too young to die.

His family all cried,
Like the waves on the tide,
Bash the sand and stones below.

Chloe Allan (12)
Plymouth High School for Girls, Plymouth

I Have A Dream

I have a dream
Of love and happiness
For people fighting in wars around the world
To stop.
To stop and remember that song
That made them smile,
To remember the words of their loved ones
That made them laugh.
To stop and remember their friends
Giggling and cheering.
For them to remember the person they loved,
That would make their hearts pound
Against their chests,
And make them grin happily.
This is my dream.

Katie Thorn (13)
Plymouth High School for Girls, Plymouth

My Poem On People Who Inspire Me

Make me a hero, make me a star,
Make me perfect, make me a car!

Make sure all children are carefree,
And see beautiful things like a bird and a bee.

Create me a hero, create me a star,
Create me perfect, create me a car!

Create a stop to bad things like war,
Because people can get hurt and sore.

Draw me a hero, draw me a star,
Draw me perfect, draw me a car!

Draw me a picture of a cuddly bunny,
In a beautiful place who is very funny.

The people who inspire me are: make me a hero,
The words that inspire me are: star, perfect, free,
Bee, war, bunny, draw, create, make.

Holly Strutton (12)
Redruth School: A Technology College, Redruth

My Mum Inspires Me . . .

My mum is my inspiration;

She works all day to please others,
She works so hard to make us happy,
My mum is my inspiration.
All her life she lives to care,
She's lived to make us learn,
My mum is my inspiration.
She teaches at schools,
My mum is so nice and lovely,
My mum is my inspiration.
She's a brilliant cook,
She tries to take us to many places abroad,
She's my inspiration.
We all have fun with my mum,
She just has the greatest smile ever,
My mum is inspiring.
That's why I love her so very much.

Kate Ashby (11)
Redruth School: A Technology College, Redruth

Imagine

I magine all the killing every day
M en and women dying
A dults crying
G iving people help
I wish it would stop, but it will
N ever happen
E arth will never be safe.

Aaron Moores (14)
Rowdeford School, Devizes

I Have A Dream - Green

I have a dream,
To see loads of green,
To see loads of flowers,
Even ones I haven't seen!

I have a dream,
To see the big, blue sea,
To see animals swim
And have fun with me!

I have a dream,
To see animals sing,
To let them be free,
To let them unfold their wings!

I have a dream,
To see the treetops high,
To walk on green grass,
Yet they never die!

I have a dream,
That pollution isn't real,
It doesn't exist,
That's how I feel!

I have a dream,
To see the shining sun,
To see all the bright rainbows,
To always have fun!

I have a dream,
It is my goal,
I want it to be real,
Not turn into coal!

I don't need fairy dust,
I don't need magic,
I only need people's trust,
So it won't end up tragic!

Blanca Gracias (12)
St Joseph's Catholic College, Swindon

Together Again

I know I'm dreaming
I have to be, I must be
The sky is gleaming
Right to the horizon, as far as I can see
And she's here, she's gone and yet she's here
Right in front of my eyes, standing before me
That's the catch, that's what makes it clear
I know I'm not awake, I can't be.

She died though, she's gone and she's dead
And yet there she is, I can see her
Picture it though, inside your head
What if it isn't just her?
Can you see it? A perfect world
Where everyone we've lost is returned
Wouldn't that just be an amazing world?
Old memories still being churned.

Your grandad, your friend, your nan
They are all waiting for you
You'll see them as soon as you can
You are missing them too, aren't you?
They can see you and are looking
They want you to live on and prosper
This place is waiting, no booking
You'll be there when you can and not before.

So whenever you feel down or alone
Don't stare at the ground not wanting to see people
Stare at the sky, the Heavens above, for although it's unknown
That's where your heart has been sent to heal
The angels above, servants to God
You'll be there one day
But not before time, it's odd
But you'll be together again, one day.

Stephanie Clayton (13)
St Joseph's Catholic College, Swindon

Me And That Child

What is the difference between me and that child?
We both have a nose, two eyes and a mouth,
We both have a body, arms and legs.
But that child lives in a dirty, broken slum,
He will never hear laughter or a mother's hum.
He has no time to play or read a book,
Poverty has him on the end of its hook.

Winner

What is the difference between me and that child?
He lives in the scorching sun, but here it is mild.
He is five years old, he is not mature,
Yet he works all day and earns nothing more,
Nothing more than a penny for the labour he's done,
No time to be a child, no time to have fun.

What is the difference between me and that child?
My body is fit, healthy and well, his body is malnourished,
It's been through hell.
The water he drinks could kill him today,
He can't clean water, there is no way.
His bones are so clear through his paper-thin skin,
No fat or muscle to protect him within,
His soul and spirit are just as worse,
He will break into pieces, he will die and disperse.

We both have a nose, two eyes and a mouth,
We both have a body, arms and legs.
I am the same as this child
But I have something that he does not,
A home, a life worth living, not forgot.
Help this child, make my dream come true,
The dream that he is helped, by me and you.

Alice George (13)
St Joseph's Catholic College, Swindon

I Have A Dream

I have a dream,
That every individual,
Big or small,
Any religion or race,
Has a special box.

This special box
About the size of a keyring
In the shape of a heart,
That people can carry around with them,
Close to them,
So that wherever they are
They will be safe.

This keyring will offer protection,
It will protect them from bullies
And racism and pain.

If you are in a place of war
It can protect you,
By stopping the bullets
And banning the bombs
And everyone gathers and becomes friends.

This special box can help you,
Find friendship,
Find a true friendship,
Find a true friendship that can last forever.

This is a special box,
A special box that could change,
Could change the world.

Caitlin Wood (13)
St Joseph's Catholic College, Swindon

Coming, Cackling, Laughing, Running

Coming
Cackling
Laughing
Running
Bright, white fangs
Dirty, brown hair
Evil smile
Wicked stare
Coming
Cackling
Laughing
Running
Down the hill
Across the moor
He's catching up
You're feeling sore
Coming
Cackling
Laughing
Running
Heel in the stomach
Talon in the eye
A screaming yell
A blood red sky
Coming
Blinking
Waking
Humming.

Donal Holliday (13)
St Joseph's Catholic College, Swindon

I Have A Dream

I have a dream,
but with each day it slips away.
I know it won't come true,
but it helps me to think of you.
You are there one week,
gone the next.
When I entered the hospital
I remember your smile.
It was the last time we met,
the smile was one
I can't forget.
You, lying helpless,
talking gibberish too,
believing we could understand you.
You held my hand
in your frail skin,
while you talked and smiled,
I nodded and grinned.
I remember when I was younger,
our trips to the market,
the look of your house
and your WWII badges.
I don't regret one minute with you,
I still cry,
but I try to be brave.
My dream is -
you're alive again.

Holly O'Hara Ball (13)
St Joseph's Catholic College, Swindon

I Have A Dream

I have a dream to conquer all others
To fly without gravity pulling you down
To shout and sing as loud as I can without getting funny looks
To just for one day not care about school
And the homework that comes with it
To walk freely along the pavement
Just following it without fear
Of who will come around the corner

So let me dream, let me sleep
Let new worlds open up around me
Let me dream, let me sleep
And be free from reality, just for a while

I have a dream to walk alongside wild animals
Tigers and lions will stroll along beside me
Birds will sing their sweet, sugary songs
Bears and elephants will roar too
Grasshoppers will jump along with the kangaroos

So let me dream, let me sleep
Let new worlds open up around me
Let me dream, let me sleep
And be free from reality, just for a while

But most of all I have a dream
That my worries will just blow away
And that everyone I know and love
Will stand by me.

Jennifer Collins (12)
St Joseph's Catholic College, Swindon

The Dream

I have a dream
That the world will be green
There'll be less gas
By using bio-mass

I have a dream
About a special cream
This cream will be a cancer cure
But to find it we need to use chemicals and more

I have a dream
That no one will be mean
There will be no more crime
Meaning no blood and grime

I have a dream
That everyone's in a team
There will be no poverty
If everyone gives money to charity

I have a dream
About a machine
This machine can clean and scrub
And maybe even cook your grub

This is my dream
I hope it comes true
It hasn't been seen
But I want it to.

Gregory Winiarski (12)
St Joseph's Catholic College, Swindon

I Have A Dream

I have a dream
It's not just for you
It's for the whole world
No poor people living on streets
Ice covers them in sheets
Sheets of ice
It's not that nice
Pain and crying
Hurt and dying
I wish they had a home
Instead they just roam
Roam around like a lonely gnome
It's a cold night
Some drunk people get in a fight
It fills the homeless with a fright
Cold and dark
The dogs bark
They shut their eyes
While wearing their disguise
Trying to hide themselves from the gangs
Because some homeless people are afraid of getting beaten
Well some of them might think they're going to be eaten.

Why can't they be like us?
They die,
We just make a fuss.

Megan Walker (12)
St Joseph's Catholic College, Swindon

Yours

I have a dream to create my own world
No difference, no poverty
Hard work for just a young girl
If only it were true
I'd create it joyfully
Like a tropical jungle through and through
Stars so visible, the sky almost white
Easily watchable during the night
Occasionally I ponder on our world's current status
With almost nothing left to explore
My world will be updated constantly
But it would always swarm with magic
No time for sadness, loss or hurt
No time for anger, or feeling down in the dirt!
The creatures would be wondrous
Cuddly, independent and loyal
The plants would be gorgeous
Bright and colourful sprouting from the soil
I would be the owner
Casting out bad thoughts
You could say that it's a bit like wonderland
But I beg to differ
I would call it *'Yours'*
This only goes to show it's all up to you
Today is it rain, sun or snow?

Jayde Woolhouse (12)
St Joseph's Catholic College, Swindon

The World

In any other world
I could be happy.
In any other world
We could live our lives.
In any other world
I wouldn't have to hide.
In any other world
We'd still have our pride.

I thought I lived in a good place,
A place I could share
With all the people in the world
And do it without a care.
But no,
We have to fight and scrap
Over the world which fell in our lap.
Only one man can own
What should be everyone's home!

So you see,
This world needs to change
To somewhere we all live together.
So we need to arrange
To end the war,
To stop the pain
And make the world whole again.

Megan Avery (13)
St Joseph's Catholic College, Swindon

I Have A Dream

I have a dream,
Dream, what a word
A word that will always exist

Dream, a word used every day
Dream on, a saying used most days
Dream

Dream, what a word
Used in Martin Luther King's speech
Dream

Dream, what a word
Dream, it's what we do best
Dream

Dream, what a word,
I dream
You dream
We all dream

I have a dream
To be a top track designer
I have this dream

Why does no one realise
That all of us have dreams?
Dream, what a word.

Connor Hunt-Preston (13)
St Joseph's Catholic College, Swindon

I Have A Dream

I have a dream that one day people of many places
will come together and hold hands and stop racism
so that everyone can get along.

I have a dream that people living in poverty
shall no longer suffer and die
because of what we are doing to the world!

I have a dream that people in the war will come home
and be happy and they never have to go and fight again!

I have a dream that when people are having bad times,
with their family or friends, at school their family are with them
through the best of time and the darkest hours.

I have a dream that people who are racist
to black people or to white people
should have to face the consequences and be charged!

I have a dream that when I wake up in the morning
I am not scared to go to school
and worry about walking along the canal!

I have a dream that my dad will stop smoking,
because I don't want my dad to die
with ruined lungs and a ruined heart,
I want my dad to die perfect, like the way he came into the world!

Sophia Viola (12)
St Joseph's Catholic College, Swindon

I Have A Dream

I had a dream
In a dream
That I was a fly
Every day people would pass me by
But then I was smushed
By a man named Bush.

Ben Mason-Edmonds (14)
St Joseph's Catholic College, Swindon

I Have A Dream

'I have a dream,'
That in the words of Martin Luther King
I have a dream that the world will be different,
That war will cease!
All will be as peaceful and calm as a dove!
Our planet will be restored to its original beauty!
A beauty so humane!
Crime will stop; there will be no hate in the world,
No one will fight
And everyone will be treated equally.
The truth is,
Can it happen?
Can war really end?
Can we re-establish our planet?
Can there really be no hate in the world
And can we really all treat each other equally?
But here's another truth,
We all have dreams.
If we can make our dreams come true
The only thing we *can* fear then
Is fear itself!
I have a dream,
Do you?

Clare Smith (12)
St Joseph's Catholic College, Swindon

Dream For Everyone

I have a dream
Not for today, not for right now

For tomorrow
A dream that life will change
Change for the good, not for
The bad.

Rachael Harris (12)
St Joseph's Catholic College, Swindon

The Dream Which Went To Dust

On the swing I swing in the summer breeze
Laughing and playing until half past seven
That's when I get home to Armageddon.
Dad is mad, Mummy is crying,
There's smoke in the air it smells kinda funny.
Screams and shouts, the smell of sick about
As my dad shouts and shouts.
Mummy is hurt, she says Daddy treats her like dirt.
I go into his room, walk over to his drawer
Open it for my eyes to see a knife and a gun, cannabis weed
Daddy sees, hits me on the head,
Tells me off and says, 'Go to bed.'
Now I'm here with an ounce on my lap, syringe in my pocket
Got a gun cocked and a heart-shaped locket.
Policeman comes up to me, I pull out a 9mm
Send bullets through his head.
Flashing lights, I feel a dog's bite
'Get down,' they scream, I fall to my knees.
Now I'm in the cell, thinking how I let my family down
I should have learnt from my father's way
To ignore it, avoid it and lock it away.
Now I gotta go, the guard shouts, 'Move!'
Gotta go to get my lunch and gruel as food.

Ross Paone (13)
St Joseph's Catholic College, Swindon

My Dream

My dream. A dream that one day I will walk the Earth;
And through the icy waters of the Antarctic
And the oppressive desert of the Sahara to reach my goal,
Mount Everest - the bully,
Travelling around the world is just the journey to Everest,
The foot of the mountain is the starting point.

My dream, a near impossible feat for me to do.
But how can I risk my life to raise money
For people in depressed areas of the world
Who are dying from a disease?
I shall tell you why, I will risk my life for these people
Because the disease is stoppable
And all these people need to stop dying are a few measly nets!
These people will be happy again and can live their lives to the full
And it will be all because of me.

My dream, it will be hard, it will be merciless - but I will achieve it
And I will climb the beast of a mountain.
I will.
For Comic Relief.
Mount Everest is like the tower of Babel
And I will make it fall before me.
That is my dream.

Will Ford (12)
St Joseph's Catholic College, Swindon

I Have A Dream

Whenever things don't go to plan,
When things end up wrong,
When I see the disaster caused,
I know that there is somewhere I can go,
I can escape to my dream.

In my dream everything's OK,
No one is horrible,
There is no such thing as wrong or injustice,
In my dream I see no threat of war,
No greedy countries after power,
Everything is equal.

But then I see the reality around me,
There are people killing,
There are countries dying,
Everywhere I look I see bad things
We don't want.

But I wish that one day my dream will become a reality,
Where everyone can be satisfied,
Where no one will have to suffer
And the good things will swallow up all the bad things.

Our dream will become our reality.

Kerry Grocutt (12)
St Joseph's Catholic College, Swindon

I Have A Dream

I have dreamed
the world is coming to an end;
I had nothing
but just my friend.
I am suffering,
talking to a rock.
They don't even talk.

Shannon Fernandes (13)
St Joseph's Catholic College, Swindon

I Have A Dream

I have a dream,
In the day and night
The reality of it
Makes my heart go tight.

I have a dream,
The world will have peace,
No one will hurt
And no one will scream.

No one will fear,
No pain will be caused
And no one
Will shed a tear.

The children will skip,
The children will play,
The mothers won't flip
And the fathers, in peace they'll pray.

I have a dream,
In the day and the night
The reality of it
Makes my heart go tight.

Flavia Seferi (13)
St Joseph's Catholic College, Swindon

I Have A Dream - Space

I have a dream
To go out into space
And go to a different place

I hope to meet some new people
And maybe to pray at a steeple
Maybe some new species
Wearing lots of fleeces

Maybe there will be a Federation
An Enterprise
A group of planets working together
On a master plan

A plan of peace
A plan of war
A plan of culture
And a whole lot more

Who knows
No one knows
Maybe there will
Maybe there won't
Let's just hope.

Harley Drew (14)
St Joseph's Catholic College, Swindon

Gangster, Gangster

Gangster, gangster
They think they're all bad
But they're not really
They're just like pussycats

They carry a knife
Or a gun
They rob a shop
Or kill a thug

Fight over territory
Or take drugs
They're off their head
With alcohol

I had a friend
But now he's dead
They killed him
Because of his skin

I hate all these gangsters
I would rather they were dead
Lucky I am still alive
But for how much longer can I live my life?

Cameron Young (13)
St Joseph's Catholic College, Swindon

My Dream For A Better Future

To change the world,
My dream you see,
Freedom in every country!

To stop abuse and bullying,
To stop the thief who stole that ring!
To stop the sexist people now,
To stop the fight, break up the crowd.

Tomorrow is another day,
Let all people have a say.
For black or white, for short or tall,
They are people, one and all.

No more homeless, no more drunk,
To save all people when their ship has sunk.
Less poor, less rich, more in between,
For everyone to see the Queen.

No more wars in all the world,
No more pain and no more hurt.
Gone forever, don't come back,
All things evil get the sack!

Marie Philippe (13)
St Joseph's Catholic College, Swindon

I Have A Dream

I have a dream no one will be left by themselves.
Every person will have the right to do what they like.
I have a dream people will never hurt or kill people
Because they think it is fun.
I have a dream for no more wars anywhere.
I have a dream for no more fear or tears.
I have a dream that people should live in peace.
I have a dream that people could change their life
And become a better person.

Anatola Henriques (12)
St Joseph's Catholic College, Swindon

I Have A Dream

I have a dream
Of one night

I'm somewhere dark
I cannot breathe
What on Earth is happening to me?

My sight grows dim
And heavily my heart beats
Like a loud cat screech

I cannot feel my arms or legs
Until I move my fingertips
I reach out and feel sand

I think I am away
But not the same as holiday
I look around and then I see

I am in purgatory
I have left my family
And now I must make up for my sins

To join them in the heavens.

Christina Mulligan (13)
St Joseph's Catholic College, Swindon

My Dreams

I have a dream that
I will be a king of the entire world
Where dreams can be true.

If I were a king
I would have a golden crown of the world
And I would have the sword of light to dreams
And if someone was bad
He wouldn't pass my dreams.

Olavo Fernandes (12)
St Joseph's Catholic College, Swindon

I Have A Dream

My dreams are a bit confusing
I wish the world was three different islands
Island one peaceful, relaxing and crime free
Island two, dark, scary and also adventurous
Island three, magical and free,
but also whatever you're thinking will happen there.

My second dream . . .
I am a famous actress/singer
I have just made number one of all time
For my song 'Wonderful World'
I have also won an Oscar for my main role
In the film 'Beautiful World'

My third and final dream
World peace!
No bullying
No more crime
No more racism

OK, I know my dreams are a bit strange and outrageous
However a girl can dream, right?

Jessica Capstick (13)
St Joseph's Catholic College, Swindon

World War

Whilst wishing to be with my children at home
And with them see the wonders of Rome,
I shoot at men and struggle for breath,
Gulping in air with the strong smell of death,
The dirt, the grime, the mud, the rats,
The enemy stalking us like cats,
There's a bang of a gun, then a pain in my head,
I touch my sore and my hand turns red,
They say the last sense you have is sound
And I know that is true as I fall to the ground.

I awoke and placed a hand on my chest
And felt my heart hammering; not stopping for rest,
The dream I'd just had was from the world war,
Where I'd lost my brother, my friends and much more,
I remember too well the sounds of the dying,
The sick and the shell shocked,
The distraught and the crying,
The hiss of the gas, the bang of the shell,
I'm still living the war and it feels like hell!

Ellen Kramer (13)
St Joseph's Catholic College, Swindon

Peace = Happiness

I don't really have a dream,
It's more of a wish.
It's not much of a wish either;
Just a desire . . .
To wash out the fire.

For peace to lead to justice,
All around the globe.
No need for a vacation
When the air holds no stress
That'll just leave a mess!

I don't really care for money;
Not really my desire.
When I have what I want
And what I need.

There's no need to please
When we can all be at ease.
Peace = Happiness
And that's all we'll ever need.

Sasha Machado (13)
St Joseph's Catholic College, Swindon

I Have A Dream

I have a dream -
That one day war will have an end,
The country Afghanistan will be rid of the evil Taliban
And al-Qaeda
And Americans and British can withdraw their troops.
I dream that one day all the terror attacks
in the Middle East will end.
I have a dream that one day
there will be peace in the world.

I dream . . .

Salik Ahmed (12)
St Joseph's Catholic College, Swindon

I Have A Dream

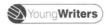

I have a dream
that citizens living in poverty
shall no more be daunted by darkness.

I have a dream
war shall be extinct and through the best of times
and the darkest of hours, after the war,
there shall be peace.

I have a dream
racism shall be a crime and anyone who commits it
should face the consequences.

I have a dream
abusive humans shall be banished,
away from humanity.

I have a dream
everyone should be equal
and no one should have more than others.

I have a dream . . .

Xavier Lewinski (12)
St Joseph's Catholic College, Swindon

My Scary Dream

Every time I fall asleep
I somehow end up dead
When I start to walk again, I am surrounded by heads
I have a knife in my hand, a gun in my pocket
Click, click, boom, then lock it.

The knife is covered in blood
I clean it as I pull up my hood
The sky is grey and cloudy
Contrasts with the blood that surrounds me
I don't know why
But I look at the sky
And something descends and grabs me
It takes me up into the clouds
And everything loud goes quiet.

Next thing I see
Is not blood and violence
It is the tears from me
On my mum's bed.

Riccardo Hillier (13)
St Joseph's Catholic College, Swindon

I Have A Dream

I have a dream
To shine like a beam
I have a dream

To beat Michael Phelps is what I want
To beat him in 100m fly
And if I succeed I will be so proud
I'll be so happy when my fans crowd

I have a dream
To shine like a beam
I have a dream

To be in an F1 team is where I'll thrive
It'll be even better if I can drive
To be a mechanic, I can live with that too
But aerodynamics is what I strive to do

I have a dream
To shine like a beam
I have a dream.

Bradley McCabe (13)
St Joseph's Catholic College, Swindon

What Kind Of Dreams

I once had a dream,
A dream so happy,
A dream so magical
I once had a dream.

I once had a dream,
A dream so violent,
A dream so unhappy,
I once had a dream.

I once had a dream,
A dream full of colours,
A dream full of wonders,
I once had a dream.

I once had a dream,
About a dream,
What kind of dream
Would I have the next night?

Alice Bailey (13)
St Joseph's Catholic College, Swindon

I Have A Dream

I have a dream that people shall live in peace
Not only could the bad people change
But the good people could become better friends
That all people will become
Citizens and homelessness will come to an end
And when you go to vote you will be able to vote
Even if you are poor or homeless.

I have a dream that I will work on a ship
And be in charge of the ship
When I walk past, people will say, 'Hi.'
I will try my best
So people will say, 'Hi,' and 'Goodbye.'

Nashwil Fernandes (14)
St Joseph's Catholic College, Swindon

A Dream Of Dreams

A dream made up of lots of dreams
Has more than just one meaning.
Like how I dream to change the world,
Or how to stop the Tower of Pisa leaning.

But now to more important issues,
Like how to bring world peace.
To stop the war and fighting,
Making murder cease.

To bring people together,
Culture, genders and race.
Stop poverty in third world countries,
Put a smile back on a child's face.

But most of all I dream
For the world to be a happy place.
Where everyone is equal,
Crime gone, without a trace.

Kaona Boam (13)
St Joseph's Catholic College, Swindon

Racism

Racism is a thing that eats itself into a person's head and starts tears
It especially affects people of a different race to us
It has affected the black people of America
It has affected Jews in WWII - most severely
It will affect people in poor countries if we don't help them
To me, racism is the worst thing in the world
Racism is not just wrong, it is evil.

Should we let racism consume this planet?
Should we let different people of religion and colour fall?
I have a dream, that one day, all races will unite and be friends
Stand up to the wrong and let the right take its place over racism
That may cause death to people.

Adam John (13)
St Joseph's Catholic College, Swindon

I Have A Dream

That dream,
The dream that I wish to always dream,
The dream that keeps slipping from my mind,
That dream.

The dream of all dreams,
The dream that's so awesome that dream will slip
your mind the moment you wake,
this dream, so illusive in my mind,
the dream will always flash before my eyes
when I don't think about that dream.

The dream will always be in your memories,
But you will not know it's there,
The dream will always be in everyone
And everyone will dream of it.
One day they will dream of this dream
And they will long to dream of it again.

Lemuel Renz Balongo (12)
St Joseph's Catholic College, Swindon

That Thing

That Thing came at exactly midnight
When it came it gave him a fright.
It scared him and he jumped out of bed
Its arms were muscular, its teeth were red.

It chased him down the stairs and through the toilet too
It even chased him when he was on the loo!
He tried to escape the Thing
The monster tried to kill him with a jewel encrusted ring.

It's life or death now, but he's trapped in a room
And that Thing now has a very sharp broom,
That Thing takes a mighty big swipe
And that Thing kills him.

Anthony Waite (13)
St Joseph's Catholic College, Swindon

No More War

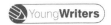

I have a dream that there would be no more war,
No more suffering, no more dying.
That children would be happy, not having to worry
If they would see their relatives again.
That they will be crying with joy instead of weeping with sadness
And that peace will stop this madness.

That they will see war is not the answer.
People should sit down and discuss their problems
Not go to war and destroy it all.
I have a dream that no more men and women should die
And that no more bombs will fly
Ending all the hard work peacekeepers have done.

So sit down, discuss, don't blow it, let it flow
So there will be no more negative flow of hateful thoughts.
Don't cause people to be destroyed
Build it up not knock it down.

Nicholas Wiltshire (13)
St Joseph's Catholic College, Swindon

Tormenting Teachers

I have a dream that all teachers
will get the right story first
before giving out punishment.

Teachers are very annoying
when it comes to homework
all they do is give homework
homework and more homework.

My dream will make school life easy
and stop people getting in trouble
for not doing homework
because we get homework
from other teachers as well.

Drew Roberts (13)
St Joseph's Catholic College, Swindon

All Different Dreams

I have dreams
We all have a dream
Some good
Some bad
And sometimes we just dream of a black sky

Some dreams we wish would be true
But some we just want to wake up
And never go back to our dream

Some sad
Some happy
And sometimes we just dream of a black sky

Some you may talk about
But some you might just want to fade away
And sometimes we just dream of a black sky

I have dreams!

Celia Ratajczak (12)
St Joseph's Catholic College, Swindon

Peace Around The World

I have a dream that
there will be peace
around the world, no more
war, no hatred.

There will be only
love and happiness
with people joining
hands together. If
this happens there
will be peace
around the world
and happiness will spread.

Agnela Lopes (13)
St Joseph's Catholic College, Swindon

Freedom Will Ring

To be free is a wonderful thing.
When you're free, millions of opportunities open . . .
thousands of possibilities dawn.

Whereas in some countries people aren't free.
No opportunities, no choices.
They are the blanks on the map.

I have a dream that one day
there will be no more blanks,
but a clean sheet for everybody to start afresh.
If we followed this path
then it will not only be me that has a dream,
but everybody.

I have a dream that today will be the dawning of a new era . . .
And freedom will ring through the halls of justice.

This is my dream.

Tomasz Skoczek & Jack Johnson
St Joseph's Catholic College, Swindon

I Have A Dream

I have a dream to save the world.

H elp the planet
A nd give all a home.
V et can help all hurt animals.
E veryone deserves a better place.

A bolish all pain.

D ecrease homelessness.
R acism should stop.
E quality is important
A nd so are you.
M y dream it is, reality it should be.

Jessica King (12)
St Joseph's Catholic College, Swindon

I Have A Dream

I have a dream that I was in a team
And all of my mates were there too
We had a laugh and went off for a bath
And also had a poo.

I have a dream that I was covered in steam
And it wasn't good at all,
So I went and had a bath and I caught a draught
And I never bathed again.

I have a dream that my mum was real mean
And she tried to kick me out,
I started to cry and wanted to die
But still, without a doubt,
She went and kicked me out.

I have lots of dreams,
Do you know what I mean?

Amber Vanhorne (12)
St Joseph's Catholic College, Swindon

What Do I Want?

As I grow up, I ask myself . . .
What do I want?

Have a happy, beautiful family
Have food that is delicious and crumbly
Have fun and exciting days
Have my children go their own way
Have meetings I cannot miss
Have alone time and one who I can kiss
Have holidays that are adventurous
Have skills and be courageous
Have a beautiful wife
Have a wonderful and great life
And I ask myself, what do I want?

Matthew Gil (12)
St Joseph's Catholic College, Swindon

I Have A Dream

I have a dream,
Like many of you have,
The world was like it is now,
The houses of brick and cement,
The small gardens with their sweet flowery scent.
I noticed some things were different,
It came as a shock to me,
When I noticed the air was cleaner,
The trees seemed healthier, a gentle green,
There were more flowers, a wonderful scene.
When I woke up I felt so strange,
I went outside and planted some spices and sage,
I brought some flowers and planted them too,
I looked down at my dress, a messy brown,
I really didn't care and continued to play
In the garden that I'd made that day.

Zoe Rose (14)
St Joseph's Catholic College, Swindon

Animals

I have a dream that all the
Endangered animals will
No longer be endangered.

I have a dream that all living creatures
That are put in zoos will roam
Free and will no longer live behind
Cages and be whipped.

I have a dream that all animals and
People will live in peace together.

I have a dream that this day
Will one day, surely come.

Ariston Lopes (13)
St Joseph's Catholic College, Swindon

I Have A Dream

I have a dream that no one is afraid
And they will never be alone.
That all of the people will have family
And a loving home.
A pathway is in front of you
And carries you through the sand,
It's like when you are quite upset
And need a helping hand.
A special friend or family
Takes that special part,
They carry you on the pathway
And are always in your heart.
Never, never, never
Shall a person be that scared,
For I have a dream that will help,
Their happiness will be shared.

Vanessa Day (13)
St Joseph's Catholic College, Swindon

I Have A Dream

My dream is simple,
My dream is true,
I love playing rugby,
I love playing football,
I kick a ball,
I throw a ball.
Bam, bam, I made a tackle,
Are they hurt?
Should I get up?
Oh look, my mate's running,
'Go on, go on!'
I shouted, he scored!

Daniel Mackenzie (12)
St Joseph's Catholic College, Swindon

Octopus

There's a dream that I had,
Wait, no dream it was, a nightmare it be.
There were octopuses everywhere.
Maybe this doesn't mean anything,
But then again, maybe it meant everything.

It was shaded in dark purple and it used dark magic
to hover over the ground.
It stretched out its tentacle which was glimmering white
I reached out; I felt I would be safer,
Then I awoke.

What did it mean? Was I meant to find out?
Perhaps the octopuses represented hope,
compassion and even love.
Maybe it showed that we could all be better.
There's an octopus within all of us.

Ryan Perkins (13)
St Joseph's Catholic College, Swindon

The Trenches

T he smell of death
H urt and can't do anything
E ntente vs alliance

T rying to move with shell shock
R yan shouting, 'Move on, move on!'
E very man working together
N ever will we cry
C arrying our guns, over the top we go
H ome, sweet home
E very shot counts
S haring our letters with each other

Blood, guts, bombs and danger
We are going to win this.

Ashleigh Loftus-Thorne (13)
St Joseph's Catholic College, Swindon

Death

I lay there thinking that day
When my daughter had to pay,
Seeing her face on that night
Still gives me a fright.
Looking over her now,
Bet she's thinking, *How?*
Who could do this thing to a child?
Bet they were thinking wild!
Police checking everywhere,
Even for a strand of hair,
I woke up from the sweat
Just to see what I had bet.
Went to check her lonely bed
And guess what?
It was not in my head.

Emma Prunty & Natalia Rajska
St Joseph's Catholic College, Swindon

I Have A Dream

S ome people don't care and are blinded by selfishness

A nother set of people help each other and are caring
and considerate
V iolent people walk the Earth with hate in their life

E nvironment is getting worse and not getting better

T his world is an unhappy place and is full of hate
H ow many people actually know about it? . . . Not many
E veryone should care about our world and it's easy to do

W ays to save the world, it's easy, just try it
O ffer the homeless money
R ecycle
L ove and care
D on't litter.

Joshua Bowles (13)
St Joseph's Catholic College, Swindon

I Have A Dream

I know I am young but I am not scared,
I have a little body inside of me
Which is a little bit scared.
Even though I shine bright the world does not mind,
I am scared of the world
But the world is not scared of me.

If you have a place to go and stay
We will find you and say,
'Do not go away,
please stay and play all day.'

Even if people do not like you,
do not worry because the world likes you,
not because of what you are
it's how you are.

Mileigh Loftus (12)
St Joseph's Catholic College, Swindon

A Dream So Merry

I once had a dream, a dream so merry
A dream that made your cheeks go red as a cherry
Did you ever want that dream to end?
Then that dream turned around a bend
It made your insides turn out
A dream that made you want to shout

Did you ever make a wish that you thought would go right
But then made you twist and turn in the night?
Did that wish then turn into a mess
That made you jump and rip your dress?

Now in the night do bad things haunt you
And make you turn all night through?
Do you now feel that you have to watch your back
Because you're going to be attacked?

Shani Altius-Ifil (12)
St Joseph's Catholic College, Swindon

Have You Ever Had A Dream

Have you ever had a dream that turned your insides out?
Have you ever had a dream that made you scream and shout?
A dream that stuck with you forever,
A dream that changed the sunny weather?

Have you ever had a dream that changed your life?
Have you ever had a dream that killed your father's wife?
A dream that made a hole in your heart,
A dream that made bad things start?

Well if you did, remember this,
Bad things will come and bad things will go,
Think happy thoughts and take things slow.
Do this and have a happy life,
Think good things
And make things right.

Lynette Mutuota (12)
St Joseph's Catholic College, Swindon

Dreaming

A dream can be a reality,
Or a time to escape the world,
When sorrow strikes,
Just a dream away . . .

It might be a daydream,
Or maybe a frightening nightmare,
But who decides?
I don't . . .

A dream can show a different view,
The better side of the world,
But when I wake,
It's not the same . . .

The world has turned upside down.

Dale Nunes (12)
St Joseph's Catholic College, Swindon

I Have A Dream

I have a dream
That some day I will become rich and famous.

I have a dream
That I could be God,
To change the world from hate to love,
From wrong to right,
From non-forgiving to forgiving,
To help *stop war!*

I have a dream
That my name could be remembered
From now until I die.

I have a dream
That someday I could be a famous footballer.

Matthew Wood (12)
St Joseph's Catholic College, Swindon

Florida

Florida is a gorgeous place, it is sunny,
You could be called funny,
When you go you will have fun,
When you go to the hotel you can run,
The place is beautiful,
Trust me on that.

When you go to the theme parks you will be all dizzy,
Trust me on this, you will end up all sissy,
You can go to Busch Gardens and others too.

When you get back home you will be exhausted to the toe,
But you can still go out and meet your friend Mo,
I'm sure she won't mind you leaving her to have a good time,
As I'm sure you will know she's done it to you so.

Lucy Farthing (13)
St Joseph's Catholic College, Swindon

I Have A Dream

I have a dream,
although it seems
things are falling down the stream.
I have a plan, to bring back my dream.

I have a dream,
to rule the world
and it's going round in a curl.

I have a dream,
that people should play music
and make a huge mosaic.
That is, if I ruled the world.

Joan Carmen Fernandes (13)
St Joseph's Catholic College, Swindon

An Ideal World

I have a dream of a world without war!
I have a dream where rich live among the poor!

I have a dream where there is food for all!
I have a dream where there is no need for a help call!

I have a dream where there's a world full of peace!
I have a dream where badness will cease!

Dreams are dreams, but reality is near,
But for all the dead will bring another tear.

This is the world that we live in,
Let's stop the badness, stop the sin!

Kieran Scott (12)
St Joseph's Catholic College, Swindon

Think

Think,
Of the people who died in wars for you.
Think,
Of the millions around the world in poverty.
Think,
Of the stacks of rubbish, piled up on streets.
Think,
And pick that rubbish up.

Remember,
Those people who died in wars for you.
Remember,
When you eat, think of those in poverty.
Remember,
When you saw that pile of rubbish on the street.
Remember,
To pick that rubbish up.

Think,
Of the years that you have wasted.
Think,
Of the things you could have changed.
Think,
Of the people who need that food you're throwing away.
Think,
Do something to help.

Remember,
Those years that you have wasted.
Remember,
The things you *should* have done.
Remember,
The people who need that food you dumped in the bin.
Remember,
To do something to help.

Think,
You can change the world.
Remember,
With words or actions you can change the world.
Think;
Anything is possible.

Tom Fieldsend (12)
The Ridgeway School, Wroughton

I Have A Dream

I have a dream,
A dream for the world,
For peace,
For love,
For happiness,
I have a dream.

I have a dream,
A dream for peace,
For no fighting,
No hatred,
No war,
I have a dream.

I have a dream,
A dream for love,
For my marriage,
For my family,
For the world,
I have a dream.

I have a dream,
A dream for happiness,
For sharing,
For caring,
For kindness,
No seriously, I have a dream!

Rebecca Lowes (12)
The Ridgeway School, Wroughton

I Have A Dream

I have a dream
That one day I could be a singer
With all eyes looking at me
I have a dream

I have a dream
Singing and dancing forever
Signing my name for whoever
It's all in my reach

I have a dream
To become famous
To not be nameless
I have a dream

I have a wish
That I could be on stage
To prove it's not just a phase
I have a wish

I have a dream
That could one day be real
How amazing that would feel
I have a dream

I have a dream
To get my picture in a magazine
With people making a scene
I have a dream

I have a dream
To appear on the TV
With everyone watching me
I have a dream

I have a dream
To have fans calling my name
Life will never be the same
I have a dream.

Eleanor Satchell (12)
The Ridgeway School, Wroughton

I Have A Dream

I have a dream
That there will be world peace
With no more war or starvation
No more murder or knife crime

I have a dream
That one day I will go to Australia
And meet my second cousins
I will also go to America for a year
To be with my auntie, uncle and cousin

I have a dream
That my best friend
Will come back from Canada
To live here again.

I have a dream
That no one would ever die
I also wish that many people I have lost
Will come back to life to see the family again.

I have a dream
That any abuse
That is happening in the world
Will stop.

I have a dream
That everyone in the world
Will be friends
With no bullying.

I have a dream
That I will achieve good GCSEs
And get a decent job
With a decent wage.

I have a dream
That there will be world peace
For all eternity.

Katie Henderson (13)
The Ridgeway School, Wroughton

I Have A Dream

I have a dream
That there was no such thing as worldwide war,
But there was such a thing as worldwide peace.

I have a dream
That all the homeless were sheltered
And were taken care of.

I have a dream
That all the racism in the world now
Was completely wiped out
And everyone accepted everyone for who they are.

I have a dream
That all races become one
No matter if you are white, black, brown, gay, straight.
It does not matter what you look like
But what's inside that matters.

I have a dream
That people don't hurt our natural community,
Recycling what you can and not just throwing it away in the bin.

I have a dream
That children don't get abused by their parents.

I have a dream
That there are no women beaters in the world
Or men beaters.

The reason I have these dreams
Is because if someone can make them turn into reality,
Then life will become a whole lot easier.

I have a dream
That these dreams come true
And if these dreams are turned into reality,
I shall ask for nothing more.

Sofia Khwaja (14)
The Ridgeway School, Wroughton

I Have My Dream

You're in my head
I can't get you out
This feeling is staying
But I just want to shout.

You said you were my father
A long time ago
But since you've been away
I just don't want to know.

I swear I loved you once
But that's all in the past
I'm living in the future
You wanted out of my life so fast.

You don't know what it's like
To lose someone close
But I've got someone loving
Who I really love the most.

Instead of calling by his name
We call him our dad
He's sweet and loving
Without him we'd go mad.

You have ruined all that trust
That was built inside of me
I was closing my eyes
And it was getting hard to breathe.

So I have a dream
I wish it could come true
But if it doesn't I will live
I will try and pull through.

Can I have my dream?

Ellie-Jay Lawton (14)
The Ridgeway School, Wroughton

I Have A Dream

I have a dream . . .
That I can see my family
Laughing and joking, together forever
But that's not reality
It's never going to be
The state of my family is a mess
And that's why most of the time I feel neglected
I wish my family were number one
Living a top notch life
But I have no problem imagining, right?

When people talk about their families
I become very ashamed
Hardly anything to be proud about
Well is there?
At times they can be cool and hip
When they're not at each other's necks
Sometimes it doesn't really matter to me
But usually I just can't take it anymore
Then again they are still my family
At the end of the day, and I love them.

I have a dream . . .
That I can see my family
Laughing and joking, together forever
But that's not reality
It's never going to be
The state of my family is a mess
And that's why most of the time I feel neglected
I wish my family were number one
Living a top notch life
But I have no problem imagining, right?

Sharon Lombo (13)
The Ridgeway School, Wroughton

Make Life Better

Why is there racism?
Why is there poverty?
Why is there brutality?
Is life worth living in this reality?

Bullets are flying
People are dying

Every day I'm with a stranger
As soon as I step on the streets
I know there will be danger

Every day I'm watching my back
Don't know when they will attack

No one is different
Everyone is the same
By being racist and by killing people
What do you gain?

Think yourself luck you got food
And you're alive
But there are other people
Don't have food to survive

So don't waste your time
Time to use your mind
If you think life's a game
Then your eyes must be blind

So let's not have racism
Let's not have poverty
Let's not have brutality
And make life worth living in this reality.

Dhiraj Budha (13)
The Ridgeway School, Wroughton

To Be Loved

I once had a dream that everybody was loved
And that everybody was treated as equals.
If I had the chance I would have stayed in that dream,
Forever hoping for sequels,

To be loved by one another,
Is the greatest gift of all,
To have that gift you must be proud of who you are,
Not tucked up, away or small,
To be loved by one another,
Is the greatest gift of all,
Whoever loves is to be loved back,
Love is the power which rules,

I once had a dream where people were killed,
All violence in towns and destruction,
Then one man stood up and cleared his throat
Then started explaining his speech production,

He had imagined a world in a land,
He explained how war should stop and how fighting should cease,
But no one would listen to his request,
Not even his protest for peace,

To be loved by one another,
Is the greatest gift of all,
To have that gift you must be proud of who you are,
Not tucked up, away or small,
To be loved by one another,
Is the greatest gift of all,
Whoever loves is to be loved back,
Love is the power which rules.

Eleanor Thompson (12)
The Ridgeway School, Wroughton

I Have A Dream

I have a dream, a dream,
To own my own horse,
A beautiful, stunning horse,
To share my life with.

I have a dream,
A dream, a dream,
To be the best I can be.

I have a dream, a dream,
To gallop along the beach,
To feel the wind, the wind,
Through my hair.

I have a dream,
A dream, a dream,
To be the best I can be.

I have a dream, a dream,
To become a professional show jumper,
To show the world,
What we can do together.

I have a dream,
A dream, a dream,
To be the best I can be.

I have a dream, a dream,
To ride a dressage horse,
To feel the difference,
And win all the dressage competitions.

Jessica Phillips (12)
The Ridgeway School, Wroughton

My Boy Billy

I have a dream,
That my tortoise, Billy,
Could be equal,
Not to be bullied by other tortoises.

I have a dream,
That one day when I leave this planet,
Billy will have a nice life with a new owner.
There, I hope they take care of him,
Just like I do,
To put an end to him being bullied.

I have a dream,
For everyone to be equal,
Not for them to be bullied,
Just because of their skin, hair or shells.

I have a dream,
That when Billy grows old and has kids,
That his offspring are treated fairly,
With all the love and care they deserve.

I have a dream,
That Billy's life will reflect on us humans,
So that bullying is stopped.

Billy is one of a kind, individual.
He is special. People should accept that,
Not hurt him because he is different.
That, is my boy, Billy.

Joshua Rowland (13)
The Ridgeway School, Wroughton

I Have A Dream!

I have a dream,
That one day,
There will be plenty of families,
Where no one's souls will be destroyed,
Where feelings do matter
And domestic violence won't happen.

I have a dream,
That one day,
There will be no more murders,
No suicide,
No runaways,
Nothing bad, for that matter.

I have a dream,
That one day,
There will be no more violence,
No more war,
No more lives lost,
No more tears.

I have a dream,
That one day,
There will be no more benefit frauds,
No more robberies,
No more pollution,
And a far better environment . . .

. . . I have a dream.

Georgia Lampard (12)
The Ridgeway School, Wroughton

I Believe!

Have you ever thought of a place
Where all people live in peace?
Have you ever thought of a place
Where all fighting will cease?

I know I have . . .

It's the place where people,
People like John Lennon
Can sing to you with no threat.

Or it's the place,
The place where Bobby Moore
Teaches you to hit the back of the net.

That's the place . . .

Where you take centre stage at the podium,
Proudly look up to the sky
And with all your might and self-esteem,
You lift your head up high!

You *are* one of these people,
You *are* one of the few,
You can be whatever you want,
You just have to believe . . .

And *make* it true!

Kristopher Banham (12)
The Ridgeway School, Wroughton

I Have A Dream

I have a dream,
That I will stay as a child,
So I won't have to experience death.

I have a dream,
That I will have a heart of amber,
So I can trap my closest flies.

I have a dream,
That there will be no wars,
So I can choose to go anywhere in the world.

I have a dream,
That pollution does not exist on Earth,
So I can be proud of Earth.

I have a dream,
That animals can speak,
So that we don't end up making decisions against their will.

I have a dream
That I can do everything that is impossible,
So that I will be noted by the world.

I have a dream,
That God opens His eyes and stops poverty,
Wars, death, pollution, racism and all affecting issues.

Thulakshia Vakeeson (13)
The Ridgeway School, Wroughton

The Planet 'My Imagination'

There is a world,
Where there is no war.
The planet is peaceful
And no one has an argument.

The planet 'My Imagination'.

There is a world,
Where everyone has food on their plate,
Where no one suffers from illnesses
Caused by starvation or dirty water.

The planet 'My Imagination'.

There is a world,
Where everyone is equal.
The black and white, men and women,
They can all play together.

The planet 'My Imagination'.

There is a world,
Where children matter.
They get looked after well
And their parents care for them.

The planet 'My Imagination'.

Rosie Hawkins (12)
The Ridgeway School, Wroughton

I Had A Dream

When I close my eyes, I see a blur
And know that fog is my future.
I want to change it, put it right,
Make where I'm heading much more bright.

For the world my first change could be
Global warming, most probably.
I think it's sad, we're killing our Earth,
If only we knew it's true worth.

Secondly, will be bullying,
There's not a more horrible thing,
To see someone picked on by another classmate
And witness the loathing and hate.

Lastly, stop smoking, it ruins lives,
Even passive smokers' health dives.
Smoking should not be allowed,
So give up and stand out from the crowd.

When I'm older and open my eyes,
I really hope for a big surprise.
Me and my dream have put things right,
Now my world looks more bright.

Caitlin Strevens (12)
The Ridgeway School, Wroughton

I Had A Dream

Love is when I loved you
Love is when I hugged you
Love is when I kissed you
Love is when you hurt me
Love is when you loved her
Love is forever
I had a dream, you, me, forever.

Shaunie Winslow (13)
The Ridgeway School, Wroughton

I Have A Dream

I have a dream
A dream to play for Liverpool
A dream to lead them
A dream to help them

I have a dream
I can lead them
I will score for them
I can't fail with a team

I have a dream
We have the team
We have the players
All they need is a leader

I have a dream
To grow old with the team
To become the manager
Oh, what a dream

This is my dream
To be with them
It won't be a dream much longer
But reality . . .

Ravi Goindi (13)
The Ridgeway School, Wroughton

I Have A Dream

I have a dream that we will all be happy
And no one in the world will be sad.
I have a dream that everyone will have food.
I have a dream that everyone will have a home.
I have a dream that everyone will be treated the same.
I have a dream that the world will all celebrate together.
I have a dream.

Charlotte Hancock (11)
The Ridgeway School, Wroughton

I Have A Dream

I had a dream
That we went away,
We went away on a rainy day
At the end of May.

That dream came true
When we boarded the plane,
And we flew away
To a country next to Spain.

We arrived in the sun
And we had lots of fun,
We drove to the beach
And I couldn't wait to dip my feet.

We were there for two weeks,
This went so fast,
It was like a dream,
They never last.

I bet you can't guess
Where I have been,
The place in my dream
Is where I have already been.

Ryan Bush (12)
The Ridgeway School, Wroughton

I Have A Dream

I have a dream,
But with no meaning,
No story to tell,
A locked door with no key gleaming.

I have a dream,
With no name,
An important lost fact,
No title that came.

I have a dream,
Yet I see no plot,
The characters have gone,
A story there is not.

I have a dream,
But how do I know?
This dream I have,
Will soon have nothing to show.

I have a dream,
That I have to keep,
This dream makes no sense,
Until I fall asleep.

Eleanor Rendell (12)
The Ridgeway School, Wroughton

Racism

Why do people judge each other
By the colour of their skin?
As it really doesn't matter,
It's the least important thing.

Close your eyes and try to picture,
A world in which we all look the same,
Without colour or variety,
Wouldn't it just be such a shame?

So with that in consideration,
Don't you feel ever so pleased?
That we are all different colours,
So why do some get teased?

What can we do to help them,
The victims of this crime?
Show care and understanding
And hopefully with time,

We will wipe out all the racism
And ignorance and fear,
So people of *all* colours,
Need never shed a tear.

Rachel Patel (12)
The Ridgeway School, Wroughton

I Have A Dream

I have a dream
That one day I will
Ride along the shore
And I will be free
As a bird on a summer breeze
There is no one else on this beach
Just me and the horse
We splash through the water
The light wind on our faces
We are both truly content
As we reach the end of the beach
We turn
Suddenly, we are cantering
We watch as the cliffs and the rock pools
Go flying by
We both want this moment to last forever
As we come back to trot then walk
We have to go now
This dream is ending.

Lizzie Hill (13)
The Ridgeway School, Wroughton

My Dream

I dream my dream
That the world is in peace,
No war, no fighting, no violence.
One beautiful time in my life,
It was peaceful
And people didn't need anything
But family and friends.
You would not need anything else.
Don't you sometimes wish
You could live in this world?

Kate Reynolds (14)
The Ridgeway School, Wroughton

I Have A Dream

I have a dream
A dream to fly the skies
This dream would make me happy
Just to soar the skies
And all over the world

Just to imagine the things
The things that anyone could do by flight
Helping the elderly
Or even the world
Crossing oceans, seas
Woods and cities

I have a dream
If this dream came true
True as true can be
Feeling the adrenaline and the wind
Shooting beyond the clouds
Or maybe just off the ground
That is my dream.

Matthew Walke (13)
The Ridgeway School, Wroughton

Think Of The People

Think of the people who are made fun of because of their colour.
Think of the people who are bullied for their religion.
Think of the people who are less fortunate than us.

Think of the people who try and try again.
Think of the people who have nothing.
Think of the people who are less fortunate than us.

Think of the people who live in a roofless house.
Think of the people who have no friends.
Think of the people who are less fortunate than us.

Kieran Hannington (11)
The Ridgeway School, Wroughton

Dreamland

Where is this land,
The land of dreams?
Is it far or is it close?
When I get there,
I will dream of what
I dream.
I wonder what my
Dream could be?
A . . .
Footie player
Or
Riding star
Or
Nurse know it all
Or
History teacher.
I wonder
Where is this land?

Laura Windel (11)
The Ridgeway School, Wroughton

I Have A Dream

If every child on every street,
Had clothes to wear and food to eat,
If all living things could be free,
To live in peace and harmony,
If every gun in every war,
Could shoot once and then no more,
If every man and every face,
Was treated equally no matter colour or race . . .

The world would be a better place.

Sam Hornbuckle (11)
The Ridgeway School, Wroughton

I Have A Dream

I have a dream
That the sun will go down at night
Without blood being spilled that day

I have a dream
That all the races can be merged as one
To be the human race for evermore

I have a dream
That all ages thrive together
Instead of living in fear
And being imprisoned in their homes

I have a dream
That the world would be young again
And pollution would cease to be

I have a dream
That people will stop dreaming of solutions
And start trying to help.

James Teeuwen (13)
The Ridgeway School, Wroughton

The Way Of Money

I have a dream that
One day the recession will end,
The economy will grow
And money will flow like a river.

I have a dream of all employed,
No poor, no rich,
No homeless and hungry,
Just with the money flow.

Will this dream come true?
Who knows?
But until then, I have a dream.

Daniel Hunter (13)
The Ridgeway School, Wroughton

A Dream Of The World

I had a dream, a dream of the world.
A dream, that we all can live together as one
And not fight over selfish feuds or indifference.

I had a dream, a dream of the world.
A dream, that war never happens
And we will not fight between ourselves
For land, religion and global domination.

I had a dream, a dream of the world.
A dream of peace,
Of what we'll never achieve.

Bodies stare towards the foreboding light,
Whilst we still fight
And that love is achieved by a bullet from a gun.
Act together and stop this, or say goodbye to the sun.

But . . . I had a dream, a dream of the world.
A dream, of us.

Andrew Hunt (13)
The Ridgeway School, Wroughton

I Have A Dream

I have a dream that peace will rule the world
And no more lives will be torn apart.
I have a dream that wars will never start.
I have a dream that everyone shall be treated equally.
I have a dream that there will be no weapons or criminals in
this world.
I have a dream that people will respect themselves and others.
I have a dream that love will never end.
I have a dream that my dreams will come true.

Julia Gurung (14)
The Ridgeway School, Wroughton

A Perfect World

I have a dream
The world will be fixed
No pain or decay

I have a dream
People can fly
Turtles can run

I have a dream
A happy dream
A perfect world

I have a dream
Frogs jump higher
Rivers run faster
Grass is greener

I have a dream
Lying on my bed
I have a dream.

Michael Palfrey (12)
The Ridgeway School, Wroughton

My Dream!

I have a dream that everyone lives in peace,
That the people will not die from diseases or war,
So violence and discrimination will all cease,
And there will be money for the poor.

I have a dream that everyone has a life,
That people don't have to live in fright,
That no one carries a knife,
So people are not worried and can unite.

I have a dream that the world is proud,
That people are not judged for how they look,
So people can speak aloud,
That life will turn back into our dream storybook.

I have a dream that people can live their lives,
So it is almost like the world is new,
That people can spend time with their children and wife,
I have a dream that my dream will come true!

Harriet Salva (12)
The Ridgeway School, Wroughton

I Have A Dream

I nventing your own world

H aving dreams is natural
A lways your own dreams
V enture into unknown worlds
E veryone has dreams

A ny nightmares you always forget

D reaming is a part of you
R esting in bed is always a good dream
E veryone has nightmares too
A nyone who doesn't dream isn't real
M y world and my dreams.

Emma Stamp (12)
The Ridgeway School, Wroughton

Utopia

I have a dream,
A dream of my own happiness,
That one day I will be king,
A king of Utopia.

I also have a dream,
About other people too.
The perfect people that would, in fact,
Live in my Utopia.

However, it wouldn't just be my Utopia,
Would it? Oh No.
To be a Utopia, everyone must be equal,
Does that make me normal as well?

Would Utopia be happiness, though?
If everyone was equal, then everyone would be boring.
Individuality is the key to happiness.
So, what really is Utopia?

Andrew Pitt (13)
The Ridgeway School, Wroughton

Do You See A World?

Do you see what I can see?
Do you see a world that used to be green grass and fields,
A lovely place to be?

Things are bad and will be worse.
Coal is burned and gases exploded,
Trees are uprooted and soil eroded.

Seas were blue but will be black,
Pollution rises, greenhouse gas is at a high.
The world is dying for you and I.

Maybe not today or maybe not tomorrow,
But one day we will all feel sorrow!

Jack Stinson (14)
The Ridgeway School, Wroughton

Now That Is What I Call A Dream

Racing the wind, heart pumping
My worries are blown away
I'm running in London 2012
I'll never forget this day!

Running is a dream to me
Watching the trees rush by
Observe the stunning, appealing views
Look at the sapphire-blue sky

Imagine the crowd, cheering and waving
My destination is in sight
Trophies and medals glistening gloriously
Shimmering luxuriously in the sunlight

Imagine the feeling of crossing that line
The ecstatic faces of the cheering crowd
I'm standing tall like I'm the head of the world
Now that is a dream that would make me proud.

Carla Huynh (12)
The Ridgeway School, Wroughton

I Have A Dream

I have a dream of a world with no boundaries

H aving the right to do whatever we please
A dream of an end to all poverty
V ulnerable countries being given
E nough food, water and medicine

A dream of happiness

D reaming of peace
R econciliation between countries
E nd of all wars
A dream of a carefree world, no
M atter what race or religion.

Emma Woodcock (12)
The Ridgeway School, Wroughton

I Have A Dream!

I have a dream,
A dream to fly,
To feel as free
As a bird in the sky.

No one can stop me,
No one would dare,
Because when I am flying,
I don't care.

My cage is open,
At last I am free,
Time to stop hoping
Because I'm free, I'm me!

I had a dream,
A dream to fly,
To feel as free
As a bird in the sky.

Lucy Mason (12)
The Ridgeway School, Wroughton

Emotions!

I have a dream

H appy
A ngry
V iolent
E motional

A nd

D readful
R ough
E xperienced
A dream
M ost of all *I have a dream!*

Chloe-Louise Watts (12)
The Ridgeway School, Wroughton

Wars

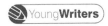

I have a dream of world peace,
Goodbye to the drone of guns,
Flashes in the night sky to cease,
Mothers can keep their sons.

I have a dream to end all fights,
To stop men worrying about dying,
To give back freedom and rights,
Let's hope everyone is trying.

I have a dream that people can see,
Families bruised and battered,
All the pain and hurt they are causing me,
Many lives left broken and shattered.

I have a dream that countries would work together,
Rather than against each other,
Best mates forever,
To treat each other like a brother.

Hannah Moxham (12)
The Ridgeway School, Wroughton

I Have A Dream

I nspiring others with what you believe in

H oping that someday it will happen
A nything is possible if you just believe
V iolence does not solve anything
E veryone is equal whether their skin is black or white

A ny dream can come true

D are to dream
R euniting black and white people together again
E njoying life as you should be able to
A mazing things can happen
M anaging to succeed even if you need to make sacrifices.

Hayley Royal (12)
The Ridgeway School, Wroughton

I Had A Dream

My dream would be:
For no racism,
What is the point of it?
All it does is crush people.
If everyone looked like you, it would be boring,
So if someone has black, white, green or purple skin,
It's their personality that really counts.
If you say something really nasty about somebody's skin,
People could take it the wrong way.

Racism is illegal,
Don't break the law.

Say no to racism.
People commit suicide
Because they get so depressed
About being bullied about their differences.

Hannah Sumner (12)
The Ridgeway School, Wroughton

A Better Place!

I dream of a better place,
Where oceans and rivers glisten,
Where there are no wars,
Where each and every person listens,
When every day is a bright, sunny day,
A place perfect in every way.

I dream of a better place,
Where every person is kind,
Where work is fun and not a chore,
Where poverty is no more,
Where everyone is united together,
United in friendship forever.

Ah, my *utopia!*

Tom Parker (12)
The Ridgeway School, Wroughton

A Greener World

When I wake up one morning,
The threat of global warming
Would have slowly drifted away.

But this wonderful day might never come,
Melting icecaps, OK for some,
We need to take some action now!
How do we do it? I know how.

Recycling, a chore,
Littering, no more.
A cleaner planet won't just arrive,
Give our planet a chance to thrive!

A greener world is a dream for me,
But I'm sure someday if we try,
It will become a reality.

Ellie Carter (12)
The Ridgeway School, Wroughton

I Have A Dream

I have a dream for when I am older,
To be that smart lady with the business folder,
To own an hotel and a business small
And when it comes true it will be so cool.
The thing I would want most
Is to live on the coast,
With visitors that come to stay,
Taking good memories away.
Every day new people to meet,
My successful business wouldn't that be neat!
When my dream comes true it will be so cool,
With my hotel and business small,
I will be the smart lady with the business folder,
Because I have a dream for when I am older.

Charlie Harvey-Jones (13)
The Ridgeway School, Wroughton

I Have A Vision

I have a vision
That the world will be at peace
To stop violence and terror
And to stop arguing.
I have a vision
That we will look after our world.
I have a vision
To lower carbon emissions.
I have a vision to look after our environment
And stop cutting down rainforests,
To stop killing, killing innocent animals.
I have a vision
To make the world a better place.

William Owen (14)
The Ridgeway School, Wroughton

Hatred/Happiness

Hatred, disbelief, sadness, loss, war.
I have a dream of no war.
None in Iraq, Russia, Darfur.
No homes burning, children screaming, soldiers killing.
That is war.

The men carry big guns,
A child desperate to escape runs.
Innocent people shot in their sleep,
As others collapse and weep.
That is war.

Happiness, contentment, delight,
But happen again it might . . .

Laura Shaw (12)
The Ridgeway School, Wroughton

I Have A Dream

I have a dream I will be famous one day,
I will rule the country and everything will go okay,
Nobody will be judged by the way they look,
Or even by reading a different type of book.

I have a dream everyone will look up at me
And they will not ask, 'Who is she?'
They will always have a huge smile on their face,
Even if they have just lost a very big race.

I have a dream I will drive around in a flash car,
And everyone will see me as a shining star.
Everyone and everything in the world will be just fine,
And they will all be celebrating with a glass of wine.

Jadene Cowan (13)
The Ridgeway School, Wroughton

Listen To Our World

Listen to the world tonight,
Dream the dreams of now,
And future dreams will come to you,
Once today is through.

Listen to the world tonight,
And it will lead you on,
Hear the bells of future time,
But not those of the past.

Listen to our world tonight,
As we depend on it,
Living life is not right,
Without our world tonight.

Sophie Rawlings (11)
The Ridgeway School, Wroughton

I Have A Dream

I wish one day all wars would end

H unger to come to a rest
A world with no more difficulties
V arious religions unite
E veryone sticking together

A mazing things to see

D ecades to go past without a crime
R acism comes to an end
E veryone being equal and fair
A life with fun and happiness
M emories can always be a good thing, no longer bad.

Ebony Patterson (11)
The Ridgeway School, Wroughton

I Have A Dream

R ecycle, recycle
E very day
C ardboard boxes and papers too
Y outh clubs are full of junk
C ans, plastic and metal too
L augh out loud, give it a go
E veryone can help

T omorrow it could be too late
O ver the moon you could be
D ance and prance and sing aloud
A ll day, every day, recycle, recycle
Y ou could recycle today!

Dean Patient (13)
Treviglas Community College, Newquay

What Can I Be?

Oh what can I be, God?
What can I be?
A mother, a teacher, a preacher, a poacher,
Or like a piece of bamboo
Swaying along with the wind?

What shall I see, God?
What shall I see?
Cities or towns,
Survival or destruction,
Birth or death,
Brothers or sisters?

What can I be, God?
What can I be?
A president or a king,
A thief or a killer,
Will I be hungry or will I be full?

Can I have dreams, God?
Please can I have dreams?
Of birds flying high,
A river of gold,
Giving peace a try?

Will I be bad or good?
It's up to you if I should.

What can I change, God?
What can I change?
Poverty or homelessness,
Rape or theft,
Racism, cruelty and all the rest?

God, have you abandoned us,
Left us alone?
We desperately need you
To heal the hurts of the world.
What can I do God, what can I do?

Cassandra Cooper-Bagnall (13)
Treviglas Community College, Newquay

I Have A Dream

I have a dream,
Around, around the field I dream, training day by day,
To run on fields and roads, but mostly in the bay.
Walking, jogging, sprinting and shouting, that's how we run,
People think it's boring, actually it's quite fun,
But when you race things can be quite a bum.

Aiming for the Olympics, taking every chance,
Popping here, popping there, dreaming to get a glance.
Hopefully when I win you would see me prance
And maybe I might *even* perform a dance.

Practising the 800, trying to make it the best,
But unfortunately there is no chance to rest.
Day by day the training never stops,
But some days I feel my body should flop.

Dreaming to be the number one,
Hopefully then I would have won.
Dreaming to be curled in my bed,
With my gold medal next to my teddy bear, Fred.

Wherever I run I dream that the sun would be out,
Which I very much doubt.
Whatever the weather I would run my best,
Even when I need a rest,
Just to be number one.

I win, I dream I am the best,
Shouting if you don't know I'm from the south west,
I am James Craddock, the number one,
Thinking that was a load of fun.

I had a dream.

James Craddock (13)
Treviglas Community College, Newquay

Noticed

Wouldn't you love to be noticed
Everyone knowing your name?
This is why I wrote this
But you might not feel the same

Everyone knew what you we inspired to do
You were special and kind
No more wondering and not having a clue
This was your chance to shine

You knew the world's aspects
You know what was going on
You knew the height of different sets
And the singings of different songs

You were out there to change lives
You helped people along
You did it without a problem
And thankfulness is the title of the song

You helped save the world
Stopped all pollution
But one thing is still wrong
This isn't a happy solution

This is only a dream
Fate can only make it come true
But maybe everyone could notice
And it will be seen by the world, everyone
And definitely you!

Natasha Scott (13)
Treviglas Community College, Newquay

Innocence

Stop.
Stop animal cruelty.
Stop their pain and sorrow.
Stop filling their warm hearts with hatred
And choose this path to follow.

Affectionate, adorable and loyal,
How can you hurt this?
An innocent, lovable creature,
This wasn't his dying wish.

You hit him, you beat him,
But what was his crime?
You punished him for no reason,
But now you're out of time.

Stop.
Stop animal cruelty.
Love them you must.
Stop abusing their loyalty
And be the one they trust.

Cute, friendly and cheerful,
Do they deserve a broken heart?
They'll stay with you forever,
You'll never be apart.

You hit him, you beat him,
You killed him.

Charlotte Jones (13)
Treviglas Community College, Newquay

Why Them?

What have they done to us?
Why do we choose them
to bully, neglect and feel the most pain?

They don't deserve the anger that they feel.
They only want one chance to live
and live real.

They're defenceless, shattered,
torn away from where they belong!
Doesn't this prove
that it is obviously wrong?

Their eyes are like scorching flames,
burning with emotion;
their hearts are empty and cold
but still full of devotion.

Look at the hell we have caused!
Look at what we have done!
Their broken hearts are just waiting
for the right person to come.

Sometimes it's too late
to break free from the nightmare and escape.
Thousands of animals die from abuse.
So let's help the many left,
to fight and break loose!

Jessica Burns (13)
Treviglas Community College, Newquay

Dental Desires

My, my dreams and I,
Where to begin,
Fascinated by teeth,
Those pearly, white teeth.
I smile all the time,
My teeth big and goofy,
I talk too much,
I gabber and gabber!
I'm crazy! My God!
I'm mad as a hatter.

My dad's fat and fleshy,
My mum is much thinner
I sing way too much,
I get on their nerves,
Over and over and over again.
Daydreaming beyond my wildest thoughts.
My dreams sweet and pretty,
Oh, what a laugh.
I love eating fudge,
But it's always gone,
Strawberry, vanilla, cream,
Do you like it too?
Let me see,
Open wide!

Amelia Fisher (13)
Treviglas Community College, Newquay

Animal Cruelty

How could you do that
To an innocent animal?
What's wrong with you,
You wicked criminal?

See the tears
Falling from the terrified eyes.
What did they do to you?
Well, how can you be surprised?

Hunting, testing and
Unnecessary murders.
There's nothing they can do.
Feel their pain - you selfish intruders.

Torture, discomfort,
Heartache and suffering.
Abused like a puppet,
Where is your loving?

Is this the last day?
Has it finally had enough?
I guess it should be relieved!
Why are you so tough?

Bang! It's pitiful waste of life -
Gone.

Hayley Allwood (13)
Treviglas Community College, Newquay

Stop Racism

Stopping racism
It's easier said than done,
We can kick it out of shops,
Throw it out of bars
And run it off the football pitch.

If we pulled together
To destroy this wretched beast,
Maybe, just maybe, we could make a better world
Where black people
May stand tall together,
Without words of hatred
That shatter our community.

Wars that have been fought for years,
May stop in a matter of weeks.
Like the fight in 1959
As the immigrants rolled in.
KBW!
Keep Britain White.
No!
Keep Britain Kind
Keep Britain Friendly
Mostly . . .
Keep Britain Integrated!

Will Prowse (13)
Treviglas Community College, Newquay

Stop Prejudice

Imagine if we left all the prejudice behind,
Imagine all the happiness we would quickly find.
Imagine if we were all the same,
No white, no thin or people in pain.
Then people wouldn't think to fight,
We would be united and always right.

Why do people see in black and white?
We know that prejudice isn't right.
Tall, short or skinny, can't you see
The person inside is like you and me?
Colour, religion, looks or creed,
Prejudice is planted like an ugly seed.
Decade to decade this hatred never ends,
Wouldn't it be nice is we could all be friends?

So stop this nonsense,
People shouldn't judge,
This problem is immense,
These people hold a grudge!

This is what I'm thinking
And this is what I'll do,
I'll make the world a better place
By stopping prejudice, without further ado.

Mary Wright (12)
Treviglas Community College, Newquay

Unknown Fiend

Towering shadows against the wall
A musty stench, everlasting.
Blood spattered, dripping, dripping,
A steel knife like a sword; malicious,
Eternally laying, staying
Unmoved.

In the dark, dark shadows,
In the dark, dark corners
Weeps a small girl,
Tears of snowdrops,
She mourns
The death of her family,
Hitting her; like a stone.

The girl emits a wail,
Chorusing agony,
Towering, waiting,
A leaf on a stem,
One more wail
Does the girl permit,
Before curling up; becoming still,
Unknown fiend.

Tertia Southwick (12)
Treviglas Community College, Newquay

Our Sense Of World Peace

Listen to the silence.
Isn't it grand?
There's no war and no grief
Right across the land.

Look at the hills,
Watch as they flow,
There's no war and no grief,
We say *No!*

Taste the pure air,
It was bitter now sweet,
There's no war and grief,
No anger, no heat.

Smell the new attitudes,
From people who fought,
There's no war and no grief,
But we still want more.

Feel the difference,
Isn't it strange?
There's no war and no grief,
We've made a *change!*

Georgina Oddy (13)
Treviglas Community College, Newquay

A Book About Love

The pen in my hand
is steadily flowing
you can't stop me now
I'll just keep on going

All of my thoughts
are now on the page
I care about writing
not about wage

My book's about love
My book's about me
I really love writing
so you can see

What I think about love
how I really feel
to your emotions
I will appeal

I really love writing
I have new-found fame
and because I love writing
you know my name.

Rosie Howard (12)
Treviglas Community College, Newquay

Peace And Hope

Peace

A world of peace would be bliss,
no fighting to be top dog,
people killed for being different,
this just needs to stop.

Open your arms and have a heart,
surely you feel their pain,
just realise we're all the same,
we're playing the same game.

Hope

If we believe we will achieve,
this world will be treated as one,
just think with your mind
and don't rewind, stay as being kind.

Hold your head up, up in the sky,
be proud of who you are,
if people sneer just give them a smile,
they know you are the winner!

Lauren O'Mahoney (12)
Treviglas Community College, Newquay

Snow-White Sorrow

A shed,
Torn; in abeyance,
Door on its hinges,
Chorusing agony
When opened

A tear in its eye,
A rope on its thigh,
Small dog in the corner,
Weeping tears of snow-white sorrow.
Fur in patches
Of majestic, sun-like quality,
Tinged blue skin
Poking through - desperate
For sunlight.

If anyone knew,
The neglect this dog was facing,
How everyone hates it,
Despises it,
Animal cruelty.

Ellie Law (13)
Treviglas Community College, Newquay

It Might, It Might

People are hurt,
So deep it's scary,
Soldiers are killing,
They're not even wary,
All we can do is hope and fight,
It will all stop, it might, it might.

The world is cold,
Not caring at all,
Shouting and violence,
Why so evil and cruel?
All we can do is hope and fight,
It might all stop, it might, it might.

We can run and run,
Wish all this would end,
This terrifying danger,
Will this never mend?
All we can do is hope and fight,
It will all stop, it might, might.

Lauren Nagle (13)
Treviglas Community College, Newquay

A Different Voice

Imagine one voice in a crowd,
A voice that makes the difference,
A life changing difference,
A difference to millions.

The death of millions,
The work of thousands,
Depends on the choice
Of just one person.

From death and suffering,
To life and freedom,
A life worth living,
A change worth changing.

A matter of starvation,
The life of a million,
Hangs in the heart and soul
Of a voice that makes the
Difference!

Chris Rae (13)
Treviglas Community College, Newquay

My Dream

Ah, what it would be like to be a rugby player,
Running in the rain without a lousy umbrella,
Up and down the pitch I would go,
Thousands of people watching the show.
It's so much better that staying in,
That sudden rush of adrenaline.
Being there for my team,
An injury or two, I'll need some cream.
All of this would make me fit,
I have to admit it would hurt a bit.
All of this, I'd be so keen,
All I'll say is stuff your football team!

Connor Morgan (13)
Treviglas Community College, Newquay

You And I May Have A Dream

I have a dream
more like many
they never come true
it's not like finding a penny.

You may have a dream
to fight the world
to free the people
of our sweet world.

I have a dream
to have a positive world
to make it right
you may get hurled.

You may have a dream
to come together
we will all be one
forever and ever.

Shelbey Adamson (12)
Wareham Middle School, Wareham

Running Free

I look out of the window and think
A few years time, perhaps.
I see them running free,
None of them collapse.

Why do we keep them shut up all day?
Some are beaten by men,
Most of them alone, suffering in pain,
They could be here, in the wild, running in a group of ten.

Jumping fences with no rider,
Giving a buck of glee,
Looking after their foals
And watching them flee.

They could run into the sunset,
Free and happy, tails held high
And running like the wind,
I think of this and sigh.

This is my dream and hopefully it will happen,
Horses have done so much for us,
Can't we give something back?
Instead of riding them, couldn't we use the bus?

Jacqueline Miller (12)
Wareham Middle School, Wareham

My Dream Is Great

I have a dream of fresh grass, green
Sprouting on our rooftops
A world of peace, for war to decrease
Where soldiers live in freedom
A land of smiles for miles upon miles
And gratefulness and eternity
A dream so great we should not wait
For a stop to all infinity.

Lily Wood (12)
Wareham Middle School, Wareham

The World

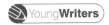

I have a dream
    that one day there will be freedom

I have a dream
    that everyone will enjoy life

I have a dream
    one day the world will be pollution free

I have a dream
    that the rivers will be clean

I have a dream
    one day the wars will stop

I have a dream
    that everyone should go to Heaven

I have a dream
    one day the sea will be wild

I have a dream
    that animals will never become extinct

I have a dream
    one day everyone will have a happy dream.

Lauren Viney (13)
Wareham Middle School, Wareham

Imagine A World

Imagine a world of poverty and violence
where our fellow man is killed and savaged for what?
For religion, for land, for riches and glory
but what divine glory is there for the killer of many?

Fame, fortune, or nothing?
Imagine a world with none of these . . .
Greed and sorrow never more.
Isn't this the dream of everyone?

Henry Moore (12)
Wareham Middle School, Wareham

I Have A Dream

I have a dream
a dream for many
to join together
so the truth we will find

I have a dream
to speak together
to know the purpose
of our life forever

I have a dream
to see the heavens
this will come true
if we all work together

You may say I am a dreamer
but there is one thing I do know
if you join me today
we can change the world
and become one.

Lisa Howarth (11)
Wareham Middle School, Wareham

I Have A Dream

I have a dream
Where the rivers are clean
And the trees are green

No more cars
No more tar
No more pollution near and far

No more crying
No more war
All this dying
What is it for?

Liam Bradley (12)
Wareham Middle School, Wareham

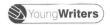

Saying No To Drugs

If you say no to drugs have a high five
Without those drugs you'll stay alive
If you take drugs you go to jail
And your face will go pale
Don't take drugs, listen to the bell
And you will not have to go to Hell
Some say drugs are good for you
I would rather eat poo
Even cocaine can blank your mind
So leave those drugs far behind
Don't take cannabis, weed or coke
It's not good for people to smoke
You may think drugs are good for you
But in fact that's not true
You can die younger
And don't eat so die of hunger
Say no to drugs they're not cool
They just make of you a fool.

Sam Johnson (12)
Wareham Middle School, Wareham

To Beat The Bully

A bully may hurt you
Physically or mentally it will hurt
This is what you can do
Physically it might be kicking dirt
But tell someone, don't keep it inside
If it's mentally, just ignore them
If they know it hurts you they will still do it
Just tell someone for yourself
Then it will stop.

Jack Speed (12)
Wareham Middle School, Wareham

I Have A Dream

I have a dream of a perfect world
Imagine a world with no one starving
It doesn't matter what colour or religion we are
I have a dream of a peaceful world
No wars around
No bombs falling to the ground
I have a dream of a non-polluted world
No factories producing smoke
No dirty air to make us choke
I have a dream of a kind world
Everyone helping each other
Everyone speaking nicely to each other
I have a dream of an eco-friendly world
No global warming going on
No electricals on standby
I have a dream of a perfect world.

Chloe Ellison (11)
Wareham Middle School, Wareham

Photographer

P icture perfect
H ow it looks
O h so beautiful
T aking pictures
O ver again
G oing
R ound the world
A mazing
P ixels
H ere and there
E diting pixel by pixel to get the best
R esults!

Oh how I wish to be a photographer!

Joanne Tsang (11)
Wareham Middle School, Wareham

My Dream Is . . .

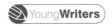

One day all this should stop
Animals no more endangered
People no longer fighting
Pollution gone forever
That's my dream

Fumes no longer choking
Ozone layer is restored
Trees are sustainable
All cars are so much greener
That's my dream

Ice caps have stopped melting
Acid rain doesn't exist
Poverty must end right now
Wasting too much should be banned
That's my dream.

Vivien Field (12)
Wareham Middle School, Wareham

Thoughts Of My Dreams

I have a dream for future, present and once past,
Of fresh, green grass and rivers where friendly fishermen cast.
I have a dream of beautiful oceans and clean sandy beaches, unspoiled, unbroken,
Of golden fields where fieldmice sleep, not to be woken.

I have a dream of lands afar,
Sparkling in the light of a star,
I have a dream of tropical rainforests,
Decorated with flowers like florists.

I have a dream of green, green land, not a house or flat in sight
And every face filled with delight.
I have a dream of little clean streams,
These are the thoughts of my dreams.

Becky Lummes (12)
Wareham Middle School, Wareham

A Mole's Dream

I have a dream that moles will have equal rights,
They will not be humans, in wars and in fights,
No more mole corpses lying on the floor
And a gun pointed at them when they walk through the door.

I have a dream, where man and mole live in peace,
Well treated with respect is better at least,
Not kicked and punched, just because it's fun,
Their tiny legs enable them to run.

I have a dream, that moles can relax,
Not have to check if there's a grenade on their back,
We should all cherish our wonderful moles,
They don't get in the way, because they live in their holes.

I have a dream, but it's only a dream,
For I am a mole and I can't afford to be seen.

Michael Selby (12)
Wareham Middle School, Wareham

A Dream

A dream is a dream with a bucketful of thoughts,
A colourful mixture, like liquorice allsorts.

A dream is a dream I would catch with both hands,
It pings back and forth like plastic rubber bands.

A dream is a dream sometimes happy, sometimes sad,
The images mostly completely mad.

A dream is a dream, imaginative and fun,
It always feels so bright and sunny like our Earth's sun.

A dream is a dream, I want it to be so real,
Then soon my sadness will start to heal.

A dream is a dream, a peaceful sleep,
Full of rainbows and rivers and dolphins that leap.

Paige Bates (13)
Wareham Middle School, Wareham

I Dream To Be . . .

I dream to be a famous singer,
I dream to be an Olympic swimmer,
I dream to be a real doctor,
or ride in a helicopter!

I dream to be a big designer,
I dream to create a new eyeliner,
I dream to own a little shop,
or be awarded a lollipop!

I dream to be an evil teacher,
I dream to be some kind of creature,
I dream to be a superstar,
or an astronaut to travel far!

I don't know what I want to do,
But I hope I gave some ideas for you!

Kate Hayward & Brittany Maxted
Wareham Middle School, Wareham

I Have A Dream

In the twilight my dream glimmers,
The moon and stars above me shimmer.
Light flows past me like a stream,
Moonlight falls in a solitary beam.

In the glade of a lonely wood,
I'd quench the stars if I could.
Then soar up to the starry sky
And dream dreams of years gone by.

I'd then come back to the ground,
With all the magic that I'd found.
But when I get up and find its fake,
I wish I never had to wake.

Amy Gwinnett (12)
Wareham Middle School, Wareham

I Have A Dream

I have a dream,
That one day there will be no wars.
I have a dream,
That one day we shall not care what colour we are,
Black, white or brown,
Does it really matter!
As long as they are a good person deep down.
I have a dream,
That one day we shall not care what religion we are,
Christian, Jew or Buddhist,
Does it really matter?
As long as they are a good person deep down.
I have a dream,
That one day there will be no homeless people.
I have a dream . . .

Catherine Senior (11)
Wareham Middle School, Wareham

The Bully Poem

He hits me
He makes fun of me
He trips me up on the bus
He does it every time he sees me

It's time to stop
The misery and the pain
By standing up to him
Before it gets worse

He went to hit me
I moved out the way
I had a go at him
And he soon backed away.

Bradley Fray (12)
Wareham Middle School, Wareham

Standing Up To A Bully

A bully is horrible,
A bully is mean,
A bully is selfish
And everything is seen.

I always told my teacher,
I always told my mum,
I always told their mum,
But he kicked me in the thumb.

I told them to leave me alone,
I told them to go away,
I told them not to bother me,
But they wouldn't go away.

Chloe Thomson & Jenny Silva
Wareham Middle School, Wareham

Beat The Bully Poem

I beat the bully on a bus
I beat him in a car
At first I didn't make a fuss
But now it's gone too far.

When he started hurting me
I didn't tell anyone about it
And I said he's just a stupid bully
If I told anyone he would start to hit.

Robbie Cobb & Robert Kelly
Wareham Middle School, Wareham

I Have A Dream

I have a dream that I could own my own bridal shop
Design the best wedding dresses in the town
I would do their hair and make-up on the day
Make sure they wouldn't look like a clown

Arrange the flowers for the bride and bridesmaid too
Amazing veils and diamond tiaras
Everything would be new
I have a dream that I could own my own bridal shop.

Amy Best (12)
Wareham Middle School, Wareham

Standing Up To A Bully

I beat the bully at rugby
I beat the bully at cricket
I beat the bully at football
I even beat the bully at running
But I never beat him up
I beat him at everything else though
I can beat the bully
But he can never beat me.

James Henness (12)
Wareham Middle School, Wareham

Greedy

I am not a millionaire
I am not a billionaire
I am not a trillionaire
I want to be a zillionaire
I want to be a gazillionaire
I wish I wasn't greedy.

Josh Green (13)
Wareham Middle School, Wareham

My Dreams

I dream of being top of the league
and scoring for Man U
I dream of being on top of the world
to get a bird's eye view
I dream of swimming with the fishes
and everything that's there
I dream of a better future
and better underwear!

Ollie Jones & Alexandro Alidir
Wareham Middle School, Wareham

I Had A Dream

I had a dream
Racism was like a chessboard
Whites take blacks
Blacks take white
I have a dream
Races were like a zebra-crossing
I had the dream
It came true.

Harry Campbell (13)
Wareham Middle School, Wareham

Standing Up To A Bully

I beat the bully at breakfast
I beat the bully at school
I beat the bully at football
So then he beat me up
I beat the bully at lunch
I beat the bully at sport
But I didn't beat him up.

Paul Dimarco (12)
Wareham Middle School, Wareham

Standing Up To A Bully

Standing up to a bully is a horrible thing to do
Do this, do that, where do I start?
Turn my brain on, I must be smart
Fighting, punching, kicking, what shall I do?
I'll go and fight alone and then say, 'B*oo*!'
The bully will run away
And I'll just have to wait for another day.

Anita Knight (12)
Wareham Middle School, Wareham

Fray

There was a man called Fray
Who had a dream one day
He was going to play for a football team
He played for Everton and was supreme
That was the man called Fray.

Liam Keggen (11)
Wareham Middle School, Wareham

The Dream Of A World

To dream of a world with no despair,
Is not a dream of fools.

The world in which we live today
Has been destroyed by those before us,
An irremovable tattoo on the breast of the land that feeds us.

To dream of a world with no despair,
Is not a dream of fools.

The world is not a monster,
It is the dreams of wrongly ambitious men that tarnish Mother Nature.

To dream of a world with no despair,
Is not a dream of fools.

To see a world with nothing but pain,
Is to see the world with eyes unopened.

To dream of a world with no despair,
Is not a dream of fools.

To hear of terror and not to care,
Makes you the guilty party.

To dream of a world with no despair,
Is not a dream of fools.

So open your eyes and open your hearts,
Care not for cruel ambition,
But dream of a world of love and peace, of joy and laughter.

To dream of a world with no despair,
Is not a dream of fools.

Samantha Clark (18)
Wiltshire College, Salisbury

Young Writers Information

We hope you have enjoyed reading this book - and that you will continue to enjoy it in the coming years.

If you like reading and writing poetry drop us a line, or give us a call, and we'll send you a free information pack.

Alternatively if you would like to order further copies of this book or any of our other titles, then please give us a call or log onto our website at www.youngwriters.co.uk

Young Writers Information
Remus House
Coltsfoot Drive
Peterborough
PE2 9JX
(01733) 890066